Why Stress Keeps Returning

Why Stress Keeps Returning
A Spiritual Response

Douglas C. Vest

A Campion Book

Loyola University Press
Chicago, Illinois

Loyola University Press
3441 North Ashland Avenue
Chicago, Illinois 60657

Library of Congress Cataloging-in-Publication Data

Vest, Douglas C.
    Why stress keeps returning: a spiritual response/
Douglas C. Vest.
        p.   cm.
    Includes bibliographical references.
    ISBN 0-8294-0713-2 (alk. paper)
    1. Stress (Psychology)—Religious aspects—Christianity.
I. Title
BV4509.5.V48   1991
248.8'6—dc20   91-13250
                                                              CIP

ISBN: 0-8294-0713-2

Dedication

I am indebted to the staff of the Institute of Formative Spirituality, Duquesne University, where I was privileged to study in 1981 and 1982 and to let my thoughts and person continue to take shape under their guidance. As I reread the manuscript during editorial preparation, I became newly aware of my great debt to Father Adrian van Kaam, who directed the institute for a number of years, and who articulated several key concepts about human formation that I have appropriated.

There is a special person to whom I dedicate this effort—the one with whom I so often share my thoughts even before I am aware that they are about to be expressed: Norvene, my friend, colleague, and wife.

Contents

1
Evolution and Stress

When Mark returned to parish work after a month's vacation, he reported to a close friend that the first two weeks away had been a recovery period for him ("decompression time" were his words). He had wandered aimlessly around the family-owned summer cottage for the first few days and had slept fitfully for the first several nights. During the second week, Mark was able to read two novels. Only then was he ready to journey about the countryside in a relaxed state. In later conversation with his friend, he confessed both his earlier fatigue and his eagerness to return to the warmth of the congregation that he served as senior minister. He had performed his work cheerfully and well for more than ten years, but on this return he felt a strong reluctance to reenter the full schedule that he believed had so depleted him of energy.

Karen has the freedom of a day off per month, in addition to weekends—a benefit of an unusually enlightened and generous view on the part of her employer! For six years, she has elected to spend most of those free days in a retreat setting, on what she terms "days of recollection." Karen describes the experience to be miraculously restorative, a gentle way of sorting out life and "getting her act together."

Her job is demanding, but its intensity does not seem burdensome because its routine is intentionally broken.

Charles retired from a managerial position in industry two years ago. He proudly reports that he has never been busier than in his retirement. Charles's wife, Marge, had long anticipated that retirement would free her husband to be receptive to travel and recreation, but he is too deeply involved in community service to allow much relaxation. "Come to think of it," Marge remarked recently, "he's smoking and drinking more than he did before!" As a matter of fact, Charles tried to reduce the amount of volunteer work several times when Marge strongly suggested a readjustment, but as he complained to a friend, he lapses into the fidgets when he is not busy.

Sam was constantly on the road for his business, to the extent that it was not clear whether he was running his company or it was running him. However, that particular problem has passed, and so has Sam—just when his career was at its zenith! Sam would have turned fifty in less than two years.

These short case histories suggest a few of the ways in which American people react to stressful life situations. More specifically, the subjects were not dealing with stress, but with pressures in the life-styles they had chosen. Karl Albrecht, a writer on issues in modern management, distinguishes between pressure and stress. *"Pressure,"* he writes, "refers to those features of a situation that may be problematic for the individual and that amount to demands for adaptation of some kind."[1] Stress is the body's response to that pressure, a response expressed in a series of biochemical reactions within the body as it attempts to make the necessary adaptation. Pressure comes from the situation; stress comes from within the body.[2]

So common and numerous are life pressures today that we are tempted simply to dismiss this serious issue with a statement such as, It's a tough world, whatever you do! Such dismissal is actually denial. So evident are the results of stress within the body that we need to cite only a partial list of physical ailments with which stress has been closely associated: migraine headaches, heart attacks, strokes, stomach ulcers, colitis, and hypertension. It comes as no surprise to find that stress is described by informed writers as a major killer in large segments of society today.

The psychological costs of stress are no less than its toll on physical health. Personal and family relations suffer from scores of pressures in our very complex world, and the societal context in which more and more people are forced to live is typified by growing harshness. Impersonality increases in our society at the very time when age-old supports of family and caring communities are disappearing. It seems, moreover, that the helping therapies cannot evolve quickly enough to keep pace with the changes and added complexities of life. Even the descriptive terms are changing; *technostress* is but one newly coined word to illustrate the highly specialized nature of some of the issues.

Is this litany of woes depressing? I fear so; but I also believe the listing has been skimpy in that it merely reveals a few sources of pressure in a general way. The news media are filled with reports and opinions about stress, though the public should be quite aware of the situation through personal observation. The question I raise is, At what point should personal concern shift from reading and hearing to awareness and action? I hope that some of the insights offered in the following chapters will help to bring about decisive change for some readers.

The Persistence of Pressure

Pressure tends to operate more often at a relatively low, persistent level than at a high, infrequent level. Its insistent nature reminds me of a day during my junior high school years when we were given sheets of soft copper from which to form shallow bowls with hammers as our only tools. First, we tacked the metal sheets across one face of thick wooden blocks into which shallow bowl-like depressions had been prepared. Then we proceeded to tap the metal with the rounded heads of ball peen hammers. We shaped the soft copper by tapping, not pounding, and after several hundred taps (which could even be done as we chatted with a neighbor), the sheets began to bulge and gradually took the shape of the depressions in the wooden blocks.

The tapping hammers in the metalwork shop provide a folksy analogy of how human beings are reshaped for better or for worse by many, many pressures or by subtle manipulations. As a simple example of the latter: For a number of years, I had my car radio set for a station that provided traffic reports every few minutes during peak travel times. (Busy freeways can be daunting with or without regular reports by observers who are happily ensconced in their studio chairs!) The favorable reports were not completely comforting, however, for I often found that the good news (an absence of highway congestion, for example) could be obtained only at the cost of being party to the almost frantic delivery of what was being said about traffic, national news, and commercial messages—all well described as "hype." This example illustrates that we are generally unaware of what is happening to our bodies and psyches in the simple exposure to what we take for granted in everyday life. (Dare I add our minds and souls to the list?) In our search for control, we are calmed by tranquilizers, boosted by mood elevators, or rescued by painkillers until we can no longer inform an inquiring physician how the body feels, for our bodies can become a sort of battlefield where chemicals strive with each other.

I hope that my readers will forgive the gloomy start. My main defense is that I am angered and wearied by the loss of more and more friends as their stressed bodies lose the battle with life's pressures. I wonder, too, how well I am handling the forces and discomforts that affect me from without and within.

The Body's Response to Pressure

A few years ago, two British writers entitled their book *Stress: How to Stop Your Mind Killing Your Body.*[3] That title gives an important but partial assessment of stress and how to cope with it in our day. But long before the burgeoning of societal pressures or the recognition of emotional factors, the human body was evolving the optimum system to deal with the terrors of natural disasters or confrontation with predators. We might term the rapid, involuntary response of the body as the fight-or-flight reaction. These internal bio-chemical processes are the legacy of millions of years of adaptation to a world quite different from the one that we now experience. It is unlikely that we shall find a quick reversal of the body's automatic physiological responses to real or imagined pressures. Moreover, our attempts momentarily to thwart what have become natural responses within our bodies will probably merely shift the struggle to another aspect of our existence.

With these general pronouncements about the body in mind, I now suggest that humankind has evolved in more ways than physiologically, and that this realization can accompany us in our search for ways of living that will greatly reduce the adverse effects of stressful life. We have evolved spiritually, for example, and rational methods of thought have explained away much superstition. Clearly, in the process of handling the pressures of living, there are spiritual issues to be dealt with—because we are quick to violate the fleshly temples in which our spirits reside—and I shall deal with some of those issues in later chapters. First, however, we need to understand how the body functions to protect itself from perceived threat.

Imagine that you are a member of a hunting tribe many millennia ago. You may imagine yourself to be either in a band of six who are hunting antelope, or one of a group remaining at the rude camp site, hoping that the hunt will be successful. You are separated from your tribe, and your senses are alert to detect the presence of food game. Suddenly, a nearby movement overhead proclaims alarmingly that a large cat is about to spring. Before you can pause to wonder whether the beast is a panther or a tiger, powerful chemical reactions begin throughout your body far more quickly than your mental faculties can decide whether to run or to stand and fight, using whatever weapon you might have.

Modern endocrinologists describe what takes place within our bodies to prepare us for fight or flight. There is a sudden activation of secretions from several glands. Within the brain, the hypothalamus initiates action of the pituitary gland, which in turn releases adrenocorticotropic hormone (which many of us know as ACTH, having been administered it to relieve the discomfort of arthritis or poison oak rash). ACTH enters the bloodstream and quickly activates the adrenal glands. Adrenalin and related compounds rush into the bloodstream, which carries these extremely potent materials to several areas of the body. In response to these hormones, the heart beats strongly and the lungs begin to ventilate more actively. The muscles receive an increased flow of blood as the more remote liver prepares glucose as food for the muscles and brain.

This is a brief description of what automatically occurs within the body when it is confronted with sudden necessity to fight for life or to seek an escape. Reaction is sudden and involves extreme changes within the body under the influence of powerful chemicals. And ironically, these rapid reactions would have taken place even if the large cat proved to be simply a combination of light and shadow moving within the tree. However, this is a good illustration of how the human body is truly conservative in protecting itself from external threat. Moreover, the body generously produces stimulants, erring on the side of caution to ensure survival and reacting even to what proves to be a false alarm.[4]

The above characterization merely summarizes how the *sympathetic* nervous system responds to a perceived threat.[5] What subsequently occurs depends upon whether the imposed threat continues. The body is ready to exert itself further to survive. Perhaps a fight ensues, in which case the blood sugar is utilized and the muscles and the several organs perform their natural functions. In time, the issue is resolved and the body remains intact but fatigued. At that point, the *parasympathetic* branch of the nervous system begins to restore the body to its prethreat condition.[6] Heartbeat and respiration rates diminish, the senses are less sharply focused, and the skin becomes warmer as blood returns from having been diverted to the muscles.[7]

The word *parasympathetic* suggests that this branch of the nervous system performs an action parallel to the stimulating branch. Indeed, the sympathetic and parasympathetic nervous systems work in an alternating or seesaw fashion; the former literally adrenalizes and activates, and the latter restores and mends. In our imagined forest situation, repeated threats would not offer opportunity for the parasympathetic system to carry out the repair function, and the body would become overstressed. A few decades ago, we might have called this unrelieved condition battle fatigue. Today, the ever-tense person (from whatever real or imagined pressure) might deprive her or his body of the ability to mobilize the parasympathetic system for needed physical restoration.

Several examples of pervasive fatigue were cited to open this chapter. What might have lain behind the brief stories? Certainly, there were no details to suggest threats so extreme as real, hairy sabertooth tigers! But as several writers have suggested, twentieth-century paper tigers also threaten healthy life. Modern pressures are subtler than those of the hunt scene and are generally more continuous or incessant (or so I believe), allowing less opportunity for needed restorative work within the body. A frequently ringing telephone can be as persistent as the ball peen hammer in the sheet metal shop of junior high school, and the summons from an unpredictable supervisor can keep an employee quite off-balance and ready for the worst case encounter at each bidding. I daresay that monitoring by modern laboratory instruments would reveal that the body responds in the stepwise secretion of powerful chemicals quite as truly on the occasion of a near-miss of an automobile whizzing past a pedestrian in city traffic as of a hunter along a jungle trail. Or, safely off the streets, we might subject ourselves to the pressure of getting consistently high grades in school. In the setting of friendship, we might feel the signal of a thrusting heartbeat, yet choose to repress the anger that is about to explode when someone deals unjustly with a family member or fellow worker.

Learning to Live with Pressure

Indeed, pressure is very much an issue to be dealt with as a matter of survival and comfort. We must responsibly treasure ourselves in perilous times—as human beings have done through the ages. And we should be remiss if we fail to note that not all stress is bad. Hans Selye, a pioneer investigator of stress who devoted much of his professional life to its study, points out that some stress is healthful. This he calls *eustress* (*eu* from the Greek prefix meaning "good"), in contrast to *distress*, which is harmful when sustained.[8] For example, thousands of fans at a football game often experience eustress together when their team is successfully moving the ball downfield. In a case such as this, stress is not an irredeemable villain. "Stress is the spice of life," Dr. Selye notes.[9] Everyone repeatedly experiences stress in the process of living. We can conceive of a range of stress that produces a high quality of life ("quality" subjectively evaluated, of course). As too much sustained pressure leads to breakdown, too little stress is accompanied by a withdrawal from life. Stress is not to be avoided but somehow to be embraced responsibly and kept in balance between that which energizes and that which fatigues.

In bringing this portion of the discussion to a close, I will review some important points.

The process of living inevitably forces us to deal with pressures.

Under life-threatening pressures, the body autonomously functions internally in a stress response.

Threatening conditions elicit powerful responses that need to be followed by appropriate restorative actions when the threat has passed.

We surmise that modern life is as pressured as life has been in former ages, though the sorts of pressure might be more subtle today.

Implied is the possibility that we can befriend our bodies in ways not sufficiently valued today.

It is the final point to which I will direct the remainder of this book. As a brief statement of my thesis, let it simply be said that, just as the physiological response to stress has evolved over a period of countless millennia, so have parallel means for restoration.

As I began this chapter with some brief case histories, so I close with another. Ten years ago, Sally and Bill invested their joint savings in a company that physically tests materials: samples of metals, strands of synthetic fibers, small cylinders of poured concrete, to name a few. One of the simplest tests performed in their laboratory determines the tensile strength of a material, how much tension or pull a sample of known initial dimensions can withstand without sustaining permanent deformation or rupture. They know that a typical sample of steel, rubber, or other material will recover its initial length after the removal of the pulling force, provided that the force does not exceed a threshold level called the elastic limit. When, however, the pulling force imposes a stress greater than the elastic limit, the sample responds quite differently. With a sufficiently great amount of tension applied, the sample will rupture. Bill and Sally know all of this about the materials that they regularly test, but they are less attentive to their own deformation under chronic pressure—both of them are workaholics.

2
Functionalism:
Productivity Out of Control

Whether or not we can verify the close connection between stress and health, most of us would readily point accusing fingers toward the seemingly unavoidable pressures with which we have to deal almost daily—and systematically, if life is to be spared the frequent changes and reversals of a yo-yo! Pressures have many sources: personal and societal, traditional and novel, internal and external. The net result is that we feel assaulted, even if a more complete awareness is delayed. Meanwhile, we may simply do what comes easily and let the rest of life take shape around that activity. For example, Mike may choose the professional course of upward career mobility, focusing on work at the cost of attentiveness to his family and community relations. Indeed, his job may seem less difficult than working out an intimate relationship or less energy-consuming than juggling scheduled periods of relaxation among the more tightly defined hours of work. Initially, the challenge might produce eustress, to recall Selye's term. In time, however, Mike will become exhausted, his health will fail, or his personal relationships will suffer. The stimulation of stress, which once energized him, will have shifted to distress.

If others in our lives appear to be imposing burdensome pressures upon us, the shift to distress might come much sooner than when the challenge is self-inflicted and gradual. Mike might explain to his wife that the career decision to work incessantly was his own, but he would object to business corporations that impose the same high level of pressure on their managers, stopping just short of exhausting the health of employees. Company managers might explain the policy as cost-effective. They receive a high level of effort from employees but do not force the breakdown of present workers, and thus they avoid the costs of recruiting and training new employees.

Social servants, notably those devoted to the healing arts or to helping people (counselors and clergy, to name but two categories), are especially prone to burnout, defined as "a state of fatigue or frustration brought about by the devotion to a cause, way of life, or relationship that has failed to produce the expected reward."[1] Less severely stressed, but skirting the risk of burnout, is the workaholic. It is not surprising that this term was coined by a therapist who has devoted much attention to counseling others fatigued by their role as helper of helpers. But workers in other areas can identify their own tendencies: "addiction to work, the compulsion or the uncontrollable need to work incessantly."[2]

Gerald May, a psychiatrist involved in private practice and hospital work, comments about a newly recognized phenomenon known as stress addiction, in words reminiscent of Mark's case story, which began the first chapter.

> If you spend prolonged periods under moderate stress, perhaps feeling tense and pressured, many of your nerve cells may modify their receptors to adjust to the increased amounts of these chemicals. The cells come to "expect" these amounts, and for the cells, stress becomes a normal state. Then, when you try to relax and find some much-needed simplicity in prayer or meditation, and

your stress chemicals decrease, the cells may react
as if something were wrong. In response, there
may be a kind of "withdrawal" phenomenon.
Something is missing, and the brain may seek
things to do or to become preoccupied with in an
attempt to restore the degree of stress to which it
has become accustomed.[3]

The Inner Urge to Keep Busy

What sort of problem is this ensnaring urge to work,
to keep busy, to do? And how does one begin to understand
or explain it? I do not propose to answer these questions
in detail, but rather to establish that it is a phenomenon
both complex and common and to suggest some underlying
dynamics. We are often quick to explain or justify our
own shortcomings to ourselves, even when we repeatedly
sense that change is needed in our behavior. Accordingly,
we may profit by first looking beyond ourselves, appropriating the clarity of being an objective viewer freed from the
subtleties of how delicately we can step around our own
risk of self-delusion. Why, for example, is a particular
co-worker or close friend working such long hours? It
could be simply that she or he has not found an escape, a
way to be the only person not following an entrenched
belief that all persons of ABC Company give extra effort or
are replaced.

An alternative explanation about a hardworking friend
might be that he or she indeed suspects that idle hands
invite the Devil's mischief, as one strain of religious teaching
insists. Yet again, our parents may have deeply impressed
upon us the conviction that the only way to get ahead
is to give extra, without making clear how much extra
or beyond what level. Then, too, we might experience a

persistent yet diffuse feeling resembling guilt when we are not perpetually busy. Whatever the reason, the result is simply that we stay in motion. Even in our home settings, outside of formal working hours, constant busyness is evident when we simultaneously eat a quick dinner while watching the evening news and scanning a magazine!

Quite evidently, countless behaviors emerge from response to life's pressures. This book is not intended to suggest explanations for individual causes and modes of response, nor will much attention be given to the many direct means of coping with stressful life-styles—chemical tranquilizers or biofeedback meters, for example. What I seek to do in these chapters is to explore with the reader several foundational elements that not only motivate every individual to act but that also can lead to excessive activity— as judged by the effect that one energizing force exerts on other forces. This interplay must be acknowledged if any of the methods can be helpful in reducing the stress reaction in an ongoing way.

Perhaps what I am about to suggest will seem to some readers little more than a change of perspective. I hope, however, that what I offer will initiate the recovery of a range of human values and responses that have evolved as truly as the body's survival response of fight or flight.

Stress-afflicted people of this age might be impatient for quick recovery from or mastery of work-related stress. The proffered cures, however, are often merely devices to displace the problem or to find a formula for short-term regain of control. A British newspaper has described how a person can monitor her or his own brain waves in order to attain self-controlled, rapid reduction of tension and to dispel the discomfort of migraine headaches or other symptoms, but also notes that this person then becomes meter-dependent![4]

What Energizes Us to Act

Four life dimensions that have evolved during the past ages (perhaps over a period of millions of years) are described in several volumes of work by Adrian van Kaam, a founder and long-time director of the Institute of Formative Spirituality.[5] What energizes a human being to do or not to do certain things?[6] We know from a very early stage in our lives that some experiences are pleasant and others are not, so we seek the former and avoid the latter. Food revitalizes the famished body, so we seek food, or we dispose ourselves to circumstances that will make obtaining and consuming food possible. This is perhaps the simplest example of the *vital* (or *organismic)* dimension. We should have little difficulty in listing scores of other circumstances that allow the experience of pleasant rather than unpleasant sensations. Certainly we would include the desire for warmth and dryness, sexual expression, slaking of thirst, the avoidance of what threatens to cut or burn, and the need for sleep even in the perceived presence of danger. These vital dimensions are expressed quite impulsively by the youngest human being. Later, as a child matures, *cultural* influences become increasingly dominant. A child seeks the company of others who respond with kindness. Certain rules of belonging or of etiquette are adopted. In times of threat to their homeland, thousands of young adults offer themselves as protectors and exhibit courage of heroic proportions in combat. In contrast, those who are not mobilized due to physical disabilities often feel unworthy or rejected, so strong is the energizing force of national crisis. These influences are cultural-historical, passed on by tradition and law, and forming much of the societal context that leads a person to conform and to feel accepted. Moreover, these types of influences vary with the times, so that what was "in" a decade ago might be scoffed at today.

Beginning fairly early in the teenage years, we begin to experience a growing emphasis on the *functional* expressions of participation in society. For a small child, the sense of accomplishment comes from the discovery that she or he can climb out of the crib or walk from one support to another, complete with the thrills of unsteady lurching and adult-applauded success. Later, a sense of achievement may come from placing the pieces of a puzzle in their proper places and still later from bringing home a good report card from school. Human beings are the most creative of animals, and there seems no limit to the accomplishments, nor to the lures or ambitions that stimulate creativity. It is on this functional aspect of human growth and formation that I shall focus for the remainder of this chapter and in later chapters.

Vital, cultural, functional dimensions all impart energy and are very much carried with us in our activities and thoughts. They are, doubtlessly, shared by God's other living creatures. For human beings there is a fourth important energizing force, subtler but more highly valued—the *transcendent* dimension.[7] Within the transcendent are the less evident expressions of life, which gently urge us to go beyond present vital impulses and functional ambitions, to relate to beauty, to aspire for resonance or union with the transhuman or supernatural. Human beings have been described as the only creatures who know that they will die and thus are able to see life as something precious. Life is not simply to be taken as a given that plays itself out in response to the vital impulses of survival and pleasure, nor is life merely doing and creating mechanically. We can transcend the basic urges necessary for survival, to receive loveliness in the forms of music and art and enter into love and longing for that which goes beyond the necessities of survival. These transcendent aspirations inform us that there is more than the immediately evident. Even the cynical writer of Ecclesiastes, after reciting a list of where fulfillment is *not*, proclaims (or complains),

He has made everything beautiful in its time; also,
he has put eternity into man's mind, yet so that he
cannot find out what God has done from the
beginning to the end.[8]

Such is the framework in which I shall consider the
place of our functional dimension, with its motivating force
of ambition to achieve. I ask the reader simply to be aware
that the emphasis on any one of the four life dimensions—
vital, historical-cultural, functional, and transcendent—
may be at the cost of neglecting the others. Emphasis on
attainment (functional), for example, might lessen a person's
ability to enjoy a good appetite (vital), whereas repeated
yielding to appetites might render one physically unable
to work (functional) or to experience the loveliness of a
natural setting (transcendent). Each dimension is intimately
related to the others, and a harmony among them is essential for truly human existence. Each dimension is important
and the four are interdependent.

The Present Dominance of the Functional Dimension

As a somewhat latter-day William Gladstone, I enjoy
swinging an axe to split wood. At times I do so for the
practical outcome of providing fuel for a fireplace. On occasion, I work out some hostilities with the axe. There are
other times, when I am at peace with myself and the
world, when my body's movement in concert with the tool
lifts me to an awareness that I am an intimate part of the
world. These three reasons for swinging the axe are simple
examples of the functional (fuel for the fireplace), vital
(emotions needing physical expression), and transcendent
(attunement to creation). Sometimes I am reminded that
physical labor conveys a sense of potency; I feel good—all of
me. On further reflection, I am aware that less rigorous

accomplishments also impart a sense of effectiveness, or of "mattering" in the created order. My response to a job well-pursued and completed is that of accomplishment, perhaps a modern equivalent of having bested another Red Knight.

On rare but insightful occasions, however, I recognize that the by-product of my functioning, a sense of potency, is only a few steps from a reveling in power. Lord Acton's maxim warns me that power, even the sort arising from productivity, might have a corrupting element. Sometimes I am lured on to more and more accomplishment, which puts me in the position of competing with a colleague. Then the reason for continued effort might become more a matter of competition than creativity, or more envy than effectiveness. Even if I am not in competition, I find that I give more and more of my attention and energy to that which imparts the sense of effectiveness. As a by-product of my work, at times I falsely feel indispensable. In this distorted view, I treat myself as a part of a machine that cannot operate without my presence. The thought seldom crosses my mind that the functions I perform would indeed be carried out by someone else should I suddenly become incapacitated. Or, if the machine analogy seems too impersonal, I might wrongly believe that I function so effectively that others, at least momentarily, are not needed—they might even become superfluous!

This description of the seductive side of achievement includes some of the dynamics that lead to workaholism, though there are certainly other factors. In one view, the experience of human effectiveness has betrayed the person. The doer becomes entrapped in a modern slavery, a thrall-dom expressed concurrently in a variety of ways. For example, the compulsive emphasis on achieving external rewards (a remunerative job or the praise of others) limits our expression in other areas of life (relationships or nonremunerative artistic expression). Compulsive emphasis on doing might lead us to invite an ongoing self-imposed context of pressure. We discover that we can "psych up" for regular anticipated crises in order to overcome them and subsequently to feel the ensuing potency. Physiologically, of course, we produce and feel the lift of the adrenalin. Repeated stress from either external or internal pressures will, over a period of time, become addictive. As experienced by Mark in the first case story in chapter 1, we might feel withdrawal when we seek to relax.[9]

Victims of Our Own Effectiveness

A friend once explained to me that the essence of drama lies in the reversal of roles. In a mystery, for example, the silent character who prefers to walk alone at night might be suspected as the thief, but late in the play the gregarious guest proves to be guilty. The one who fit the stereotype of innocence proves to be the one who does a destructive turnabout. Or, we recall that Cinderellas of all centuries can change from housekeepers into palace-dwellers, and captive frogs can turn into princes—the stuff of ever-popular stories and the bringers of hope. Clearly a turning point of monumental importance for countless people is the Resurrection of Christ, a most dramatic shift in which the crucified victim of a religious conspiracy becomes the rescuer of humankind!

Returning to our intense worker, we can see the possibility of a switch in roles. The ever-present, hardworking proprietor might, because of failing health, prove to be the victim and, in moments of insightful honesty, admit that he placed the burden upon himself, that he was the persecutor of self.

My childhood was enlivened by being present several times in the enthusiastic audiences at melodramatic performances on Ohio River showboats. The fair lady whom circumstances threatened with all manner of calumny seemed at first clearly destined to become victim, though in my heart I desperately hoped that it would not be so. Her very name itself always bespoke encouragement, both for the victory of virtue over vice in a general sense and for her personal rescue from the sleazy, unprincipled villain whom the audience booed as with one voice. All the while, there was hope that the well-named, well-built, well-motivated rescuer would prove to be just that, and that his selfless defense of the lady would have its gratuitous reward in a romantic finale only begun on stage.

It was melodrama that I witnessed on the boats. The outcome was known in advance and the art form (if that description be not overstatement) was characterized by exaggerated theatricality. Our movement through life is more like drama than melodrama, for the final outcome is not clearly perceived. Life is more like a great tragic play, because we are not offered only the clear choice between good and evil, but between two goods (though in concept it could be two evils). Life may be dramatic, but it is seldom melodramatic!

Why doesn't a good day's work have its built-in reward? In many cases, it does. But in other instances, the villainous element delays entering the drama until our creative, energizing functioning becomes functionalism.[10] Then, the functioning becomes the focus for life. We classify each other by our work, beginning acquaintanceships with the question, "And what do you do?" As Adrian van Kaam writes, we "totalize" our doing side. We should not be surprised if we experience life as partial, an important point that I shall explore later.

Questions to Ponder

But for now, let us pause to question ourselves about our own tendencies. Do we find a sense of achievement from what we do? (I would hope that this is so for all people!) Are we becoming dependent on that doing, living our lives as if our personal worth lies in our doing? Has this dependence gone so far that it has become our nature to be hastily doing, so that others come to see us as constantly in motion and we ourselves are uncomfortable if we are not active? Have we given such emphasis to activity that our functioning is fairly described by calling it an *ism*—often used disparagingly as a suffix but nonetheless descriptive of what we may have come to treasure?

In biblical times, prophetic voices would liken such a strong commitment to a single expression of life as idolatry. Such a focus is often found in our commitment to work. In our time, theologians remind us that God is the creator of all and that we human beings are given the freedom and means to be cocreators. In the focus on our great creativity, along with its many positive aspects, lies the risk that human arrogance will lose sight of the shared nature of creative acts, forgetting that we are cocreators. Thereby we risk loss of a precious relationship with the author of life. We can, in short, come to believe that we can do without God.

I invite the reader to consider a few questions before proceeding—questions that focus on the comfort or discomfort in releasing the urge to stay busy.

What pressures keep me active when I would prefer to relax? Examples might be that there are deadlines to be met, or that I am under pressure from a superior who controls my job security. I might want to attain a quota in competition with others or desire to surpass my own record. Or, I just might want to prove to someone that I can keep producing when the going is rough! Now a barbed question: Do I keep moving because it is more pleasant at my workplace than in my home? In any case, it is most important to name the pressures, to know what accompanies the energetic expression, even when the preference is to relax.

What constitutes relaxation for me? Is this relaxation restorative, or does it, in fact, make me uneasy because a task will be waiting when the rest time has passed?

What are my most frequent thoughts when I am not busy? (If you have read this far, dare to write some words as you let your mind free-associate on the question, allowing at least ten minutes after you have relaxed from reading.)

The following is a three-part question, also to be written.

1. How much would be enough for me? One or more of the following: enough money, time, challenge, recognition, affirmation, love, life?

2. Am I a person who genuinely enjoys long hours of work? If so, have I recently wondered whether pleasant eustress might give way to distress?

3. Could I convince a wise person who knows me well that my view of enough is realistic?

To raise one more question (and others can be raised and personalized by the reader): Is it true that where we place our emphasis in life is likely to be the locus of pressures that subject us to stress because, relatively, other areas are less attended? There is, obviously, a ranking of values in our lives—what we do has antecedents in what we want. In our age, the elusive dimension of time is the best measure of our values in life.

3
Time: Then and Now

Clocks, which once brought regularity and order to life, are now considered heartless taskmasters by those who scurry to meet obligations, to reconnect with loved ones, to begin cross-country travel, or simply to eat while on the move. We bind timing devices to our bodies in the form of wrist-watches, some of which update the time every second as dim lights flash from their small faces, suggesting that not an instant must pass unrecorded. Altogether, our way of life is inseparable from monitoring the passage of time.

To tidy our lives in weekly and monthly cycles, we carry appointment books, which may, ironically, contribute to pressure. We might say, "The next few weeks are jampacked, but I can give you half an hour two weeks from next Tuesday." But our unspoken message could be, "I just can't bear to have blank spaces on my office calendar, so I make sure that it is usually full." Our use of time indicates what we emphasize in our lives and can point to the origins of pressures that engender stress.

When we think of time, our thoughts often turn to devices of human construction. These measurers are, of course, based upon the physical rotation of the earth: Clocks and watches recall that fact by the way in which their two pointers traverse a circle. Whereas for eons much of human

23

labor was dependent upon natural cycles of the earth in relation to sunlight, we now have means to illuminate and warm or cool our factories and shops so that we may indeed work around the clock.

Time has come to be valued very much like a commodity. We conceive of time as something that can be saved or wasted or lost. Its close connection with productivity has begotten the expression "Time is money," meaning that time can be used in such a way as to be transmuted into money.

Beyond the world of production and finance, we conceive of life itself as ultimately regulated by a certain amount of time, which is allotted to each of us. Very near the surface of our thoughts there is often a fear that we might run out of time before something or other is accomplished. There is an anxiety that we might, because time is limited, prematurely deplete a precious allowance, namely life itself. Consequently, we subject ourselves to a variety of pressures that falsely promise that we might find a way to rescind the threatening verdict of the ongoingness of time.

Time, then, is viewed not only as a commodity but also as some sort of container. This view raises questions such as: How much activity can I fit into the next _____. (Fill in any word as long as it is a unit of clock or calendar time.) We rush ourselves, pressuring our bodies into a stress response if the larger hand of a clock moves too near to a particular marking on a dial. We do, indeed, suffer greatly from "hurry sickness," as an unrecalled writer has noted! It may be that we are merely trying to avoid peak traffic—to find a "window" in time for the quickest commute to the workplace while a small crisis at home has the impudence of occurring too near the optimum moment for departure. For example, I endeavor to allow extra time so that I do not leave home in a rush. In a hurried state I can usually feel the muscles of my forehead tighten, a reliable indicator that my body objects to the pressure imposed. The quickness with which the tension makes itself known suggests that I live close to a limit. The instigator of an early morning crisis might be one of our cats who has rested the night out-of-doors and has darted through the just-opened door evidently hungry and impatient. The cat's body wants food, but my body was already in motion for the freeway and now my glands are probably secreting as much adrenalin as if the pussycat were a panther.

Note that I unthinkingly recorded the words "extra time," as if I am given a reward for good advance planning. Indeed, it does work out that way, for departure five minutes earlier will net an arrival fifteen minutes earlier than if the insouciant cat happens to claim the five-minute margin. My inadvertent use of words such as "extra time" reminds me not only that I have been extensively acculturated about time, but also that I have uncovered still another modern view of time, namely, time as the measure for distance! For example, my office is located about thirty-five minutes from my home if the cat sleeps in, and almost fifty minutes if he seeks my hurried attention.

The tiger images—fleshly or paper, real or imagined— point up the challenge of programming in advance the need for time, of reserving some time to accommodate the unforeseen. If my activities are poorly planned, villain Time moves in. Maybe my upcoming presentation before a gathering of colleagues needs just a bit more attention. I am grateful that I stayed up late the previous night to finish the work—but what if the copying machine is not working when I arrive? My concern about punctuality imposes that pressure and comes out of my imagination.

Thomas Merton, a writer and Trappist monk, has written that busyness is the most rampant form of violence today. We could debate how much of anything is necessary before it becomes rampant, and we might have somewhat different views of what is violent, but Merton's perception correctly describes the world I have known.

Let there be one more accusing finger pointed at Time. Our interactions with it leave us in the position of feeling caught between day-to-day concerns about wasting time and the longer-term wonderment about whether we have been working compulsively. In my home desk is a reminder of the urge to stay busy: a pocket-size calculator that reverts to a timekeeper when its switch is moved from the "calculate" position. I recollect a statement by the philosopher-theologian Martin Buber that suggests that the real nature of the Hebrew captivity in Egypt preceding the Exodus under Moses was that the people had accommodated to the life-style of the land and times.[1] The Hebrews were partly oppressors of themselves, in Buber's view! So it is in some of our settings today.

Is Life or Time Central?

Can we now agree that modern life is time-centered? If it is so—if, for example, time often is given priority over even health—do we not need a new view of time and self, specifically of how each is valued? David and Evelyn Whitehead, writers on continuing education for ministry, have sounded such a concurring opinion in an essay entitled "A Christian Asceticism of Time."[2]

A modern example of our time-centered living is provided by the digital watch on whose face the current time is illuminated, courtesy of a battery (no winding necessary), a tiny quartz crystal, which does the measuring, and a compact display face, which reveals the time. I am informed that some children who know mainly digital timekeeping (and time allocating, we may surmise) do not have a good perception of daily and longer history. There are no moving hands as on the so-called analog clock or watch to suggest the passage of time from past, through present, to future.

It is not only the very young who are not able to fathom time. St. Augustine (died A.D. 430) commented that if nobody asked him about time, he understood it, but if an inquirer asked him to explain, he realized that he did not understand.

What is time? Who can readily and briefly explain this? Who can even in thought comprehend it so as to utter a word about it? But what in discourse do we mention more familiarly and knowingly than Time? And we understand when we speak of it; we understand also when we hear it spoken of by another. What, then, is Time? If no one asks me, I know; if I wish to explain it to one that asketh, I know not.[3]

Our modern views of time would startle the ancient Hebrews, whose lives were closely linked with the natural movements of heavens and earth rather than human-made devices. In the ancient Hebrew language, there is not even a general word for time nor any special words for categories of time. Ancient Hebrew verbs are treated quite differently from those in the modern languages. Though action is very important (indeed Yahweh is a god who acts!), the reader of old Hebrew scriptures is aware of verb tense from the context of a sentence. In language as well as life outlook, time was conceived of quite differently from the modern view. On the holy mountain, Moses engages in dialogue with Yahweh near the burning bush. When Moses pushes to learn the name and identity of the divine authority who is sending him to Egypt, Yahweh responds, "This is what you shall tell the Israelites: 'I AM has sent you!'" (Exod. 3:14). Footnotes often explain the translation as "I am what I am" or "I will be what I will be." Past, present, and future are bound together, but the intention is clear—the God of Being is sending Moses on a most important mission, which will lead to a new form and quality of life for the tribe.

Hebrew grammar reminds us that the biblical view of time and life was quite the opposite of the way in which we deal with existence nowadays. We tend to treat life as if it is time-centered, whereas the Bible reminds us that the reverse is true: Time is life-centered! This difference between biblical and modern views is evident in the fact that the New Testament, which was originally written almost exclusively in Greek, uses two words to describe time. In English, these words are transliterated *chronos* and *kairos.*

The concept expressed by chronos pertains mainly to duration or intervals of time. For example:

> For a long time, [the demoniac] had worn no clothes. (Luke 8:27)

> I shall remain with you for only a short time now. (John 7:33)

> This grace had already been granted to us, in Christ Jesus, before the beginning of time. (2 Tim. 1:9)

> I have given her time to reform. (Rev. 2:21)

The Greek word *chronos* enters the English language in such words as chronic (of long duration), chronicle (the recording of events in history), or chronometers (measurers of time, such as clocks or watches).

Though its derivative words are common today, chronos is used less in the New Testament than another word for time. The word commonly employed to describe the dynamic nature of history and life events in the New Testament is *kairos,* for which there is no derivative in English. The New Testament writers prefer it as the word best suited to convey a sense of the "proper moment" or timeliness with respect to one's life, God's plan, or a decisive historical event. Some examples of such opportune moments are:

> It was at this period [time] that Moses was born. (Acts 7:20)

> My words will come true at their [appointed] time. (Luke 1:20)

The time is near at hand. (Luke 21:8)

At the appointed moment [time] Christ died for sinful man. (Rom. 5:6)

[Our Lord Jesus Christ] at the due time will be revealed by God. (1 Tim. 6:15)

Note that there is quite a different relationship between event and time insofar as the two New Testament words and underlying concepts are concerned. As an example, consider the expected birth of a child. Of the several persons involved—baby, mother, and midwife or attending physician—it seems that the child best "knows" the proper moment for birth. Others might be very aware of signs of the imminent birth but, barring force, the adults must await the moment (kairos). This is quite different from a (pardon the pun) preconceived thought that the gestation period for Homo sapiens is about two hundred seventy days, and consequently that the child will observe that generalization precisely to the day (chronos).

Another moment of fulfillment (kairos) can be noted in the hobby of vegetable gardening. The package for Silver Queen sweet corn suggests that the ears will be ready for the cooking water in ninety-two days. That estimate is an average expectation, for the day of first fruits depends upon weather and other conditions. I am happy to state, as a matter of fact, that in the year of this writing the succulent ears of Silver Queen rushed ahead of the seed pack's prediction and came to the table before the scheduled date.

Viewed from biblical ages to the present, the perception of time has moved from a general consensus about an interrelatedness—and thus interdependence—among God, nature, self, and others to a contest between self and something that can be measured (chronos time). Measurement implies control; but since an individual cannot control a variety of internal and external forces, we tend to assume responsibility for the situation—and to feel the resultant pressure. Altogether, the shift over the centuries has been from the sense of appropriateness and plenty (the cup of life overflowing) to the present-day situation of our days being crammed full.

Where Does Time Go?

Now, lest this chapter be confined to impersonal discussions about time, I invite the reader to "take time" to evaluate her or his current view of time and life. The following steps allow the reader to learn how she or he currently deals with time.

> List the major categories of your activitites during a typical day. You might, for example, elect to consider a typical workday. (If you prefer a suggested listing of categories, hold on for the next paragraph.)
>
> Assign hours (or fractions thereof) that are involved for each category during your typical day.
>
> Do not total the listing of hours assigned.
>
> Review your list of categories and assigned hours until you are comfortable with them. The time involvements should faithfully describe the way you are living.
>
> Now add the list of numbers to determine a total of time assignments in one day.

If you have chosen to wait for the promised list, here are some suggested categories:

MAJOR TIME INVOLVEMENTS IN MY "TYPICAL" DAY
A modern look at chronos

ACTIVITY	HOURS
1. Sleep	——
2. Food: eating, preparation, cleanup, marketing	——
3. Work: outside the home, at home, other (e.g., volunteer labor)	——
4. Travel	——
5. Recreation: physical other	—— ——
6. Study	——
7. Initiation of personal relationships	——
8. Child or adult care	——
9. Community involvement	——
10. Spiritual nourishment (prayer, worship, meditation, other)	——
11. Introspection (life planning, evaluating the quality of life, other)	——
12. Other	——
TOTAL HOURS:	——

Very likely, your typical day is not an exact twenty-four hours in length. Ponder silently whether there is some helpful message in why the total hours in your typical day is not twenty-four. Also, consider whether you are satisfied with the proportions among the categories (e.g., whether there is too little time for recreation or personal relationship, or too much for another category).

Whereas chronos has been presented as a measure of the typical or habitual, I now offer an exploration of kairos in terms of the exceptional or occasional moments that, in retrospect, might prove to be life's turning points. The charting of clock time was suggested above as one way to explore chronos in daily life. The more informal and free-flowing evaluation I now suggest offers the reader an opportunity to explore possible experiences of kairos in life. To begin, gently reflect on the following list, noticing items that evoke a resonance or recollection in you, and then explore your response. The examples may assist you to recall moments when kairos signaled important realizations.

A friend appropriates an idea or concept only after she has heard it expressed for the "umpteenth" occasion. Apparently some internal preparation on the part of the hearer was required before "the time was right"—before the idea really could be understood, as if the idea and something interior needed to meet. We might wonder about ourselves, also, whether we have experienced this seeming slowness in learning an important lesson. If so, we can begin to realize that some learning cannot be forced, no matter how much pressure we might apply for rapid appropriation.

We experience the solitary breaking in of an insight when we are not consciously thinking about the particular subject. It seems, on such occasions, that several hours of information arrive within several seconds of clock time. Often, we are especially receptive while in a warm tub or otherwise caught off guard. This periodically occurs for me when I hike alone, and for that reason I carry with me a pencil and paper to note the insights for subsequent reflection or journaling.

A seemingly chance remark proves to be most helpful to another person—though it may only be a throw-away line by the speaker of a lecture or dialogue!

We are precipitously released from a nagging habit, such as a cold turkey freedom from smoking after having "quit" numerous times in the past.

We suddenly realize our own fragility and preciousness, perhaps at witnessing a birth. In such a case, we move from witnessing an event to valuing life itself.

We greatly value a few minutes of time with a loved one, in contrast to an hour or so with a casual acquaintance. These moments can be so precious that we leap forward in expectancy, eager for the next meeting.

Certain turning points can be seen best in hindsight and are more to be accepted than explained. The happenings just were! At the time of their occurrence, the events seemed unimportant, but in retrospect we value them as major turning points in life.

This final example of kairos is a good point from which to move into quiet reflection or journaling, listing three or four events that seem to have been important turning points. Such events might first come to mind as treasured memories that return persistently but gently. When a list has been completed, make a second list of those rites of passage that are often considered by society to be key events: marriage, graduation, release from the armed forces, or obtaining the first major job. Very likely the first listing will be more valued than the second.

Obviously, our life experiences can help us to distinguish between chronos and kairos. We are largely regulated by the former, but treasure the gifts of the latter. We long for more time with loved ones and seek to facilitate the attainment or repetition of moments of warmth.

Nowadays, one hears the expression "quality time"—scheduled moments when two or more individuals seek to be specially present to each other in ways that kairos might be more likely. For example, a busy professional person might be totally absorbed at the workplace from early Monday morning until mid-afternoon on Saturdays. Part of Saturday and all of Sunday are available for the family, and within this block of time close contact is sought. The intention is commendable, but the result might be disappointing unless all participants are receptive. We might say that kairos for all of the principals needs to coincide. In any case, this meeting often takes the form of the usually busy person offering an attractive activity, which is not lightly declined, and all become caught up in some form of recreational busyness. Alternative outcomes might be exhaustion for the overworked one or tolerant (perhaps cynical) inquiry by the others: Are we having fun yet?

The desire for fullness and quality is not to be put aside lightly. I hope that these comments about two quite different concepts of time in the New Testament have given the reader some new insight about how our views and use of time strongly bear on our ability to deal with both life's pressures and life's pleasures. Concern only with clock time suggests that we strive to exert considerable control, whereas awareness of the timeliness of life events that seem to defy our immediate control point to the need for our receptivity. These two realities can perhaps be valued most readily in our willingness to use chronos (especially in removing our concern about wasting or losing time) in order to let the timeliness of kairos be evident in our lives. In the process, we might come to value more and more the centrality of life, rather than time.

4
Work: Friend or Foe?

For the readers who paused to complete either of the suggested inventories of chronos time, work probably claimed a major number of hours in a typical day, as sleep might take the lead in a typical week. Chances are that few people would carry on animated conversation about sleep, but we could easily encounter many opinions about work. Some comments might border on the effusive, "I just love it!" while others might be a terse combination of, "It's a job" and, "Thank God it's Friday!"

A recent newspaper article advised something like this: Take a good look at your job; ask yourself how much work you are doing, and how much work is being done *on* you. Then it predictably introduced a commentary on boredom, stress, and reduced productivity in the workplace. I was reading this account while alone and was thereby spared hand-wringing or lapsing into the temptation of conversing with someone on a variant of "Ain't it awful?" (to recall one of the games people play while avoiding true dialogue). Had such talk ensued, at least one of us probably would have commented about the entrapping nature of work—though an outside arbiter would have been required to clarify whether the trap was in fact the work setting, a burdensome home mortgage, a personal choice to live at a level of particular style, or the lure of a generous pension.

At one extreme in the spectrum of opinion about work, some of us would be quick to cite the assembly line as a place where work is done at a rapid pace—work upon the workers as well as on the objects being produced. A depressing view of the moving production line suggests to us a sort of war of attrition in which the almost-stationary worker completes one limited task only to confront its twin, the same connection needing to be made or item applied on the skeleton of a creature soon to be born some yards distant.

Other persons in our imagined discussion would take their stand elsewhere in the opinion spectrum, some opposite that of the assembly line worker. Dorothy Sayers, of mystery story and theology renown, for example, commented during her radio broadcast "Living to Work":

> When I look at the world . . . I find myself dividing people into two main groups according to the way they think about work . . . One group . . . look[s] upon work as a hateful necessity, whose only use is to make money for them so that they can escape from work and do something else. The other group—smaller nowadays, but on the whole far happier—look[s] on their work as an opportunity for enjoyment and self-fulfillment.[1]

Sayers made clear that her sentiments lay with the second group; work is not essentially what she does to live, but what she lives to do. Her statement reminds us that there are down-to-earth reasons for holding particular views; these reasons challenge her outlook as being a privileged one. The sole wage earner for a large family might have quite different reasons than a single person; a well-trained person's reasons might differ from those of someone who is unskilled or disabled or highly trained and willing but suddenly unemployed because new management eliminated all positions in a branch office.

Glancing for a moment from the worker to the product, we are reminded that the worker is not the only determinant in the workplace, for created things take on lives of their own, though not always so dramatically as in the assembly line example. A worker can become dependent upon her or his machine or appliance in the same way that a life routine can be set by one's own business. A company's organization chart takes on a life of its own and from time to time persuasively announces, I have a vacant spot; please fill me. Even the unvoiced expectations of participants in a voluntary group such as a church can sway the life of the congregation, whereupon the urge for the group's solidarity takes priority over the significance of its individual members.

Religious Views of Labor

Biblical views of work do not help a great deal to clarify the long-standing and strange relationship between humankind and labor. The opening chapters of Genesis, for example, swing from an invitation to tend a fruitful paradise to a punishment levied in the form of sweat required to bring forth food from the earth. From the New Testament record, we have formed the image of Jesus as a working carpenter. St. Paul reminded his audiences that he supported himself by the labor of his hands, being gifted with the skills required for making tents or ships' sails. He also commented that work allows people to have food for distribution to others who are imprisoned, on pilgrimage, or suffering famine. Ironically, in seventeenth-century colonial America, Captain John Smith quoted one of St. Paul's letters to the infant church at Thessalonica when he asserted that "who does not work does not eat" (2 Thess. 3:10). And shortly before Smith's time, John Calvin (a leading theologian for the Protestant Reformation, and perhaps unwittingly a theoretician for capitalism, as well) wrote,

> Let each one abide in that calling [St. Paul, 1 Cor. 7:20]. This is the principle from which other things follow; each should be content with his calling, and persist in it, and not be eager to change to something else.[2]

Unfortunately this rationale is too facile for the interclass distortions when capitalism is functioning at less than its best!

We could, after spending a few hours in a good library, have a sizable listing of respected writers who have called upon Scriptures to discuss whether work is a means or an end, with fairly equal numbers preferring each view. Those who believe that work should be seen as an end in itself might argue that work has intrinsic worth and should not be devalued as merely a means to gain something else, such as material items or prestige, while the labor that provides the means is not respected and the worker is devalued.

Those who believe that work is not an end might say that it should be done for the glory of God. Some might even assert that work should not be performed for personal reasons alone (nor for one's own glory!), but is to be performed with and for God. The "with God" notion would be readily accepted by agrarian societies who depend greatly upon nature's gifts of land, sun, and water. Their celebrative offerings at harvest would point to the "for God" view as well.

Once we sort the many opinions, we are left with some helpful insights worth reviewing in any age.

> A person's self-worth should not come from his or her work—not from work to person.

Personal dignity can, however, come through dedication to a chosen occupation, from what the person brings to the work, somewhat the reverse of the above. The worker dignifies the work, so that even the humblest occupation may bring dignity.

Daily occupation should be treated in such a manner that it ennobles the person. In that way, a value not easily found elsewhere is added to labor.

In the view that labor is at its best when building the Kingdom of God (with all of the interpretations of what it means to let God's will and ways truly prosper!), we can glimpse an important truth: Our work is most fulfilling when its focus is beyond individual gain and even beyond the benefit of a narrow interest group.

Work can be seen not only as an outward expression of ourselves but truly as an ongoing completion of ourselves.

The last comment brings us to reconsider the biblical account in Gen. 3:1–19 and comments offered by the British educator-ethicist David Attwood.

God continues to care for the earth, but he gives to man the responsibility to dig the soil: 'God took the man and settled him in the garden of Eden to cultivate and take care of it.' When man fails, the soil is cursed among other things. 'It shall yield you brambles and thistles, and you shall eat wild plants. With sweat on your brow shall you eat your bread until you return to the soil as you were taken from it.' This is the heart of the matter. Work is good; God worked and man shared in God's work, but this has been spoiled. Man is entrusted with great responsibility and invested with great dignity—his work should reflect this and express his true relationship to nature and to his fellowman. The dignity can be lost and the responsibility misused, but this does not affect the central affirmation about the goodness of work. Work remains both necessary and good, although subject to frustration, decay, imperfection. It needs to be redeemed.[3]

Another attitude toward work has been common within monastic communities for about fifteen hundred years. Monastics have not found all of the answers to work issues, but they are governed by specific guidelines that could help workers who lack both a supportive structure of acceptable guidelines and the personal reinforcement of a caring community. Therein, in other words, can be found a shared sentiment about daily life together, in which manual labor has been considered a necessary ingredient but not the major one. The example I shall use for illustration is that of Benedictine communities, for the simple reason that I am more familiar with their views than those of other monastic communities.

The Benedictine perspective emerged from the experience of predecessor groups at the beginning of the sixth century A.D., after ancient Rome had been overrun several times and humanness had largely disappeared from the Western world. Beginning then and continuing for perhaps six centuries, civilization was restored owing in large part to the growth of monastic hostels, hospitals, schools, libraries, and orphanages.

It has been said, perhaps in a somewhat partisan manner, that civilization was restored because the monks continued daily to sing the several divine offices of prayer. Another convincing explanation advanced is that prayer and work were bound together, as indeed they are in the motto of Benedictines: *ora et labora*—prayer and work. A better reason is that the three elements of prayer, study, and manual labor were all emphasized, even to specifying the numbers of hours to be devoted to each involvement daily. Thus, care of spirit, mind, and body were recognized at the outset as necessary for wholeness of the person. Prayer, study, and work were interwoven to eliminate artificial constructs that separate the spiritual from material.

This view is made explicit in chapter 43 of the *Rule of St. Benedict*:

> On hearing the signal for an hour of the divine office, the monk will immediately set aside what he has in hand and go with utmost speed, yet with gravity and without giving occasion for frivolity. Indeed, nothing is to be preferred to the Work of God.[4]

This directive is not intended to devalue work in comparison with prayer (which is viewed in the Rule as the "Work of God") but rather to emphasize the need for a balance of the two. The manual tasks will still be there when prayer is finished. Meanwhile, the community comes together in prayer as well as in labor. Prayer, even private prayer, is not something for which the individual is solely responsible. God is very much involved in all prayer! So it is also that God is involved in work, sustaining the worker and workplace on the earth.

Such, then, are a few of the views of work arising out of religious tradition. In a more succinct way, let's note some measures of the importance of work.

> Work is necessary for survival. It provides food and other necessities either directly or indirectly from the specific labor.

An individual's harmony with society is dependent in large measure upon whether she or he is carrying a fair share of the labor. For example, persons on welfare are often judged adversely even when an inability to work is the basic cause of their dependence.

Not only are there many expressions of work, but there is also great variability of ways in which work is experienced and valued.

If work is persistently boring, the individual may conclude that not only are personal gifts being unused and unappreciated but life itself is being wasted.

If work is engrossing, the worker may be oblivious to the plight of those less fortunate, or be so absorbed that other important issues in her or his own life are undervalued.

Underinvolvement in work can lead to apathy, and overinvolvement to hyperactivity.

Society's status ranking of some forms of work over others can lead to devastatingly lowered self-worth.

Long-term deprivation of the opportunity to work (e.g., by reason of unemployment) dramatically illustrates a wide range of what has just been listed—from concern about survival to low self-esteem.

What Is Work?

Our discussion of work to this point has presumed an understanding of what is meant by work. Mark Twain, in *The Adventures of Tom Sawyer*, wrote: "work consists of whatever a body is obliged to do, and play consists of what a body is not obliged to do."[5] A dictionary describes work as "activity in which one exerts strength or faculties . . . to perform something . . . to overcome obstacles and achieve a result."[6] According to such a definition, professional football players and sod-busting farmers would all be engaged in work. But, what about neighborhood children playing football in a schoolyard, or a weekend gardener eager to finish digging the flower bed so that seeds can be planted? The worker's perspective of the activity is obviously very important in shaping her or his perspective of work.

Our life experiences give further insight about work. We might discover that what is laborious for some people is recreative for others, or that the views of an individual change according to circumstances. We can come to enjoy work that we formerly disliked, or to have the opposite experience. I now propose to examine four expressions of work that I have experienced in the hope that readers will gain insight into their own past and present work. The four types of work are job, vocation, avocation, and hobby.

A job suggests income, a way of filling the day, fitting into someone else's desires and time schedule. We speak of a job market and expect remuneration for an assigned job adequately performed. A substantial job might be called a task, and a minor one a chore. Overall, the objective, the compensation, and the time limitations are specified. A job is usually clearly separated from, or even valued in opposition to, the other activities of life.

A vocation envisions a somewhat different entrance into the experience of work. The word carries with it a sense of being called, urged, summoned, or invited to a particular function or task. Details might initially be less defined than those of a job. The church has been perceived as preempting use of the word and opening the way for a two-level view of Christian people, some individuals being invited to special status and others not. My view is that some people are as convinced of a call to be homemakers as others are to be clergy. In any event, initial response to a lifelong commitment is often typified by a mixture of certainty and uncertainty, and the decision is encouraged by new energy, which accompanies continued movement in the direction that resonates with a person's deepest feelings about how life is to be spent.

However definitive the sense of vocation, it must be lived out within some sort of human construct—a community or organization—and thus the full expression of a gifted person is not always possible in a particular religious congregation, hospital, home, school, or elsewhere. The gifts possessed by an individual might strongly lead her or him to a given profession, but an organization chart calls for somewhat different skills and interests. God might urge, but a parish or industrial superintendent requires! For these and other reasons, an avocation (the third face of work) can gracefully complete the expression of gifts that allow the individual to feel fulfilled creatively. This avocational work is pursued in addition to a person's usual occupation, more out of a desire to feel expressive than for remuneration. (In contrast, moonlighting is usually more for the purpose of gaining extra income than for sharing gifts.) The individual will need to discover an avocation that resonates well with her or his gifts and perhaps forgo pay as a volunteer tutor, as a creative writer, or in another labor of love.

Except when I have been caught up compulsively in a job or vocation, a hobby has provided an essential way for me to feel in harmony with part of the created universe. Whether diversion, minisabbath, or recreation, several hobbies have allowed me to transcend the usual. My basic motivation has been more longing than one of anticipated reward. Moreover, my hankering has been more than psychic, for all of me feels good when I have been gardening, working with wood, or kneading bread dough—affirming my resonance with simple tactile experiences. When my hands are thus occupied, my mind seems recentered. And, happily, hobbies allow failures more readily than do the other forms of work.

Looking at the four faces of work has been informative for me, and I wish to share some of my insights. I have looked too simplistically at the issue of work in the past. Salary from a job is not sufficient reason to submerge other expressions of my energy, for example. My life has provided other insights.

> It is misleading to try to extract from any one of the four types of work more than it can provide. A job seldom can allow me to proceed at my own pace; a hobby seldom provides sufficient money to pay the mortgage or utility bill. (The same principle applies in other aspects of life. It is unrealistic to expect all interpersonal needs from a single relationship—or all respite from the burdens of work by repeatedly getting away in travel.)

> Immersing myself in more than one of the work expressions points to the value of balance in the rest of life. Harmony can profitably be sought even when a balance is not immediately realized.

> My urge to express (most sharply illustrated by the concept of vocation) is not simply to do, but to be in relationship with God, others, and myself.

> Presence plays an important role in the midst of work (or all else in life!). Presence to myself is as important as completing the task. If completion is regularly my goal in any of the four aspects of work, I should reconsider my choice. Obviously, a

relaxed presence is most easily possible with a hobby, but even there a garage filled with unfinished tasks bespeaks a lack of attentiveness to self!

The breakthrough to self-presence at its best can be in the regular expression of thankfulness—giving thanks that I am able to do manual labor, for example.

Work cannot stand alone! The importance of balance in life reminds me that the issue is work and nonwork in harmony—*ora et labora.*

Total loyalty to one or more of the expressions of work will not carry the day, either! When I feel that a deep personal interest is unexpressed, it is probably because what I have viewed as loyalty to the work has been at the cost of a loss of expression in some longed-for aspect of life.

I am more important than what I do!

New perspective does not merely inform me about how my work ranks with other issues of life but can also start me toward harmony.

An anecdote from an essay entitled "Working for a Living" illustrates my assertion that a person's dominant view of work depends very much upon how she or he approaches it.

Two Zen monks [were] both prodigious smokers. Concerned about the question of smoking during their prayer time, they agreed to consult their superiors. While one received a stern reprimand from his abbot, the other was given a pat of encouragement. The unlucky one, greatly puzzled, asked his friend exactly how he had framed his question. "I asked," the second monk replied, "whether it was permissible to pray while smoking."[7]

5
Restlessness: A Spiritual Signal

Two decades ago, the words of a wall poster made me aware that "Life is not a problem to be solved but a mystery to be lived." This was a gracious encounter, for I continue to realize that living well is not only a matter of mastering successive situations but also of appropriating their mystery. We cannot deal with stress simply by identifying problems and going to work on the sources of pressure. Even if we could meet each challenge that is thrust upon us or that we create, we would eventually discover that the progression of problems to be solved never ends. We could spend a lifetime constantly reentering the contest of problem-solving. More important, we could impoverish our lives by denying the enriching presence that mystery brings to our life experiences. The issue is not forceful or even subtle mastery but gentle appreciation of mystery.

I recall a conversation, just a few years ago, with a young British couple who were waiting to occupy a table that my wife and I were vacating in an English restaurant. One of them, noting our American accents, asked what we were doing in England. I replied that we were studying and writing at a residential library in Wales. It was a new idea to them that someone could live in a library, and both of them showed immediate interest in my ideas about stressful life and professional burnout, especially long-term responses to these problems. Both bombarded me with questions, but only the woman seemed ready to listen. Though the man posed several pointed questions, he repeatedly interrupted my responses. His summary comment was, "My dad never succeeded in life. I'm afraid of failure. Whenever things aren't working out, I go on the attack." He apparently confirmed his wife's great concern for him, for she exclaimed, "And when you're that way, your face is droopy and tired, and you look twice your real age!"

As our conversation continued, I began to suspect that the man perceived life's challenges not only as immediate problems but as lifelong enemies, and that his response was not an occasional fight or flight, but a continuous brawl with life. More moderate in my later judgment, I concluded that he represents a large segment of humanity who believes that sufficient money and human resources can meet any challenge, from landing people on the moon to eliminating a contrary national ideology in another part of the world. When this attitude of defeating problems by sheer determination and effort is applied to elements of life that are basically mysterious, the result is often further exhaustion. The restless struggle then becomes more and more a matter of physical and mental fatigue, which hinders further thought about alternative solutions. Addictive stress and professional burnout often have such a genesis.

The Temptation to Keep Moving

Sometimes we discover that the answers we seek become more elusive as we become more active. The American psychoanalyst Rollo May has sagely observed, "It is an odd and ironic habit of human beings to run faster when we have lost our way."[1] I have been physically and mentally active for most of my life and, for many years, moved from one interest to another. Yet, only in witnessing the similarly active life of one of my children (who also seemed to be in constant movement for almost three decades) did I realize that both of us had physically acted out the search for our place in this enormous universe. This active pursuit, rather than a way of coping with life, might instead have been flight from the immediacy of life already being lived!

The constant search can forestall our asking deep questions and being receptive to the insights that might follow. I recall a conversation with five other persons in which we considered life after retirement. As a group, we were unable to deal with the question, for the discussion repeatedly reverted to consideration of what we might do. The concept of being was not discussed on that occasion, for the topic either was not comprehended or was avoided. Since then, I have concluded that we can hold off questions about just plain being for a lifetime. A large highway sign reinforced my conclusion—Quicksilver Village: Retirement at Its Most Active.

I encourage the reader to pause and reflect on the major way in which she or he addresses life—whether by fight or flight. What seems to be fight might indeed be a form of avoidance, or flight. More desirable is a means of coping that has been thoughtfully adopted and is generally free of extreme measures. Responding silently to the following two groups of questions might give the reader initial direction for reflection.

Do I tend to mobilize additional resources when an obstacle remains between my objective and me? Am I able to release the problem before physical exhaustion forces cessation? For example, can I both feel and say, "I'm running out of gas," and then stop the effort for a period not defined at the moment of ceasing? Do I view myself as a good team member who persists among more energetic others even when I am about to drop with exhaustion? If I should decide to quit when tired, could I withdraw without feeling guilty?

Am I, on the other hand, more likely to stay in motion, but express myself within a new endeavor that seems to restore the vitality lacking in the old activity? Do I engage in the new activity for restoration or escape? If I am seeking escape, can I break the cycle by stepping back from busyness? Would I seek to replace the old activity?

There are scores of ways to restore vitality, some helpful in the long run and others not: adopting a new hobby (we can be creative after work, at least!), engaging in physical exercise, taking courses at a nearby school, beginning a love affair, relying on chemicals, or (in extremity) redecorating the house or having a baby. Each choice momentarily works for certain people, and they seem to have new energy or perspective. Some efforts might prove helpful in an ongoing way; others are temporary in their helpfulness and may have high withdrawal costs. But all might momentarily bring energy and potency, thereby restoring the vital dimension that fatigue obscures in the busyness of functionalism (our devotion to doing).

Of course, we may choose to neither increase effort in our major means of expression nor move into an absorbing new involvement. We might elect to let life remain at status quo. In any case, pondering the situation is recommended, for careful appraisal will likely be the starting point for a new perspective.

Our Fundamental Unrest

Counselors often hear questions that bear on the deep wonderments and yearnings of life, such as:

Is this all there is to life?
Am I missing a connection somewhere?
How do I get off this merry-go-round and start over?

Thoughtful persons also volunteer summary statements of concern:

I should be content. After all, I have a faithful spouse, a healthy family, a lovely home, and a good job. I really should be content, but . . .

Sometimes I wonder if I am being unfaithful to myself.

At times I just know that the real, the old me is still inside.

I'm in the midst of people, yet I feel alone and unnoticed.

These questions and confessions arise in both stressful and relatively unpressured lives. Women and men ask them, both persons settled in their religious faith as well as individuals who give little conscious attention to the transcendent. I have concluded that these and related deep questions and concerns about our existence arise in all persons who allow themselves to ponder life. The removal of pressures in life will not eliminate our deep wonderment. Thus, in our discussion of stress, we need to consider this seemingly fundamental form of unrest along with the more immediate and identifiable sources of pressure.

Persons who are deeply concerned about a persistent restlessness might seek competent help in the search for whatever seems to have been lost or never found. This assistance could include counseling, meditation, and a host of other aids. Although the counseling arts have restored deeply disturbed people to relatively normal life and have attained a well-earned respect in society, I believe that our restlessness cannot be allayed by discovering the psychological roots of our discomfort. Nor can we do justice to the restlessness by diversion, nor by forceful adaptation to our circumstances of place and time within the world. Neither vital nor functional dimensions (alone or even together) have the capacity to help us understand and respond to these transcendent questions. St. Paul correctly reminds us that our citizenship is not solely on earth.[2] Earthbound responses to life's deepest questions are too limited for our full human expression.

St. Augustine further illuminates this in his often-quoted affirmation, "You have made us for yourself, O Lord, and our heart is restless until we find our rest in you" (*Confessions,* Book I, section 1). His fervent statement is pregnant with implications! We too were created for relationship with the transcendent. We are capable of relationship with the divine. We are given a restlessness in the depths of our being; we will remain restless until we accept rest in the transcendent, until we are drawn beyond ourselves and our personal and human limitations.

Perhaps St. Augustine concluded that his restlessness was not simply a product of present circumstances. Rather he sensed a deep yearning for union with God, which would affirm and continue to shape the sense of uniqueness received from his Creator. Such a sense of specialness could not lightly be thrust aside. Nor was St. Augustine the only person to whom the specialness of his origin is revealed. The Bible cites a number of poignant examples. In the Book of

Jeremiah, the young prophet-to-be resists Yahweh's summons to enter a life of calling people to responsibility and hope. Jeremiah's youth is the basic defense for his resistance. God's response is clear—Yahweh has known Jeremiah even before the latter was given self-awareness. "Before I formed you in the womb I knew you, before you were born I dedicated you" (Jer. 1:5). Six hundred years later, St. Paul had a similar realization. He wrote, "The time came when he who had set me apart before I was born and called me by his favor chose to reveal his Son to me" (Gal. 1:15).[3]

An adult confronting the awesomeness of God experiences simultaneous attraction and desire to withdraw from the divine one. The confrontation can be unnerving, as it was for Isaiah. God comes to Isaiah, who is in the depths of human grief and depression: "Woe is me, I am doomed! For I am a man of unclean lips, living among a people of unclean lips; yet my eyes have seen . . . the Lord of Hosts!" (Isa. 6:5). For others who have been even marginally aware of God's involvement in their being from earliest life (e.g., Jeremiah and Paul, and perhaps a majority of us), the reaction is not fear but resistance and ultimate acceptance. This combination of hauntedness ("Wherever I go, you are there, [God]!") and acceptance are lyrically combined in the 139th Psalm. Verses thirteen and fourteen are a short reflection on the many ways in which God is aware of the writer's being. "Truly you have formed my inmost being . . . I give thanks that I am fearfully, wonderfully made"(NAB).

Searching for One's "Real" Self

The Psalmist is but one writer in Scriptures who praises God's presence in our lives from the beginning of our existence and the divine Origin who creates each of us as originals.[4] God is a creator who knows us as we really are— and that is more than we have discovered about ourselves! Perhaps this ongoing search is an important cause of human restlessness. We sense an urge but do not follow and allow ourselves to discover what God has created within us. Indeed, we might resist the admission that some essence of the divine does reside within us.

I have often wondered how I might go about discovering the real me. Many persons (psychologists, for example) would point to the past, saying, "Here are some of the experiences that formed you, that made you who you are today and suggest how you will respond to future life situations." Another might agree and add, "Even more than the formative experiences of the past, your genes closely define the 'real' you."[5] Several years ago, a physician measured my blood pressure and reported, much to my pleasure, "Just like that of a teenager." I responded in playful relief, "Yes, I try to maintain reasonable habits, live cleanly, and have regular exercise." His friendly retort was simply, "Perhaps, but one of the smartest things you ever did was to make your specific choice of ancestors!" Certainly our genes, like our past experiences, are influential in forming the present person.[6]

Several times I have fantasized about being a participant in the television show "To Tell the Truth." On that program, three special guests each sought to convince a panel that she or he was the person of stated identity—the real Myrtle Meyers, for example. Each guest would state, "My name is Myrtle Meyers," and then the panelists would question each of the guests. In time, each panelist would guess which of the three guests was, in fact, Myrtle Meyers. In my fantasy, the guests are the three "me's." The first to speak says, My name is Doug Vest. The speaker is the "ought-to-be" Doug, the one whom I have been encouraged, taught, manipulated, nurtured, or even threatened to be. My fantastic thoughts, taking a hint from real-life objection to many "shoulds," would quietly rejoin, But that's not the real me! That's the one others wanted me to be!

The second Doug in my fantasy is the "want-to-be" Doug. Sometimes that is a Walter Mitty-type person and sometimes one who is willing to be less manic than Thurber's sea captain, ace flyer, brilliant surgeon, or exceptionally debonair individual—all in one person! In any case, I have since discovered that the "want-to-be" me in real life would have been rather elusive, changing by whim from month to month. Then, of course, there is the third Doug—the genuine article, the "real" me. But in or out of fantasy, I have never been able to give a good description of him. In later years, I have concluded that my fantasy needs not three, but four guests to make the game authentic for myself. That fourth person would be the "original" Doug, the one God knew before I was formed—and knows even now.

St. Augustine's confession, "You have made us for yourself, O Lord," can be very helpful if applied to ourselves. Our hearts are and will remain restless until we find our rest in God. Our restlessness can often be considered a trustworthy signal that the God who has created us is still around us and still cares. The nature of the divine care is very personal: One expression of that concern is that each one of us is truly an original. No one else has ever been or ever will be exactly like us. We can accept the fact that no two sets of fingerprints are identical, but in far more profound ways, as entities, we are each different from the other. We can think in terms of uniqueness, or one-of-a-kindness. Uniqueness suggests to me not simply oneness about which I can be proud (justifiably or not), but also a mild warning that no other human being will ever be able to understand me fully. Such understanding of me from beyond myself will be only by God. Uniqueness suggests, alas, that I must always feel alone.

The Restless Search for Self

The gist of my argument is that our elemental but pervasive restlessness arises out of our lack or loss of appreciation for our original selves. I speak not simply of the loss of childlike innocence that is often followed by a hardened view of life but of the absence of a fundamental relationship without which life lacks an essential source of vitality. We are restless because we don't know who we really are; we cannot know who we really are except in the context of an ongoing relationship with the God who created us.

In van Kaam's model of four dimensions of human formation, a life lacks the transcendent unless it includes a childlike openness to God. We need to move beyond the creaturely dimensions of vital impulses, cultural conditioning, and functional motivations to include aspirations for the transcendent. Although we can function as creative persons, feel vitality arising from several sources, and be good citizens in the sociohistorical setting, we can nevertheless languish as human creatures without the transcendent to lift us beyond mere creatureliness. The pervasive restlessness that often takes the form of a hauntedness continues to remind us of the absence of and our need for the transcendent in our lives. In that sense, restlessness is a helpful spiritual signal. It keeps before us the sense that something is lacking in our lives, and that the void has not been filled by the best efforts or diversions we have been able to muster from any human resource.

The restlessness that we have been considering suggests an unrecognized presence of the divine. The persistence of that restlessness gives some assurance, in the words of a hymn, "love that will not let me go."[7] The poet Francis Thompson describes God's persistent, faithful presence in "The Hound of Heaven." The poem opens with

> I fled him, down the nights and down the days;
> I fled him, down the arches of the years;
> I fled him, down the labyrinthine ways
> Of my own mind: And in the midst of tears
> I hid from him.

The end of the poem signals a new awareness with a clear description of human fear, fatigue, and final union.

> Now of that long pursuit
> Comes on at hand the bruit;
> The Voice is round me like a bursting sea . . .
> > 'All which thy child's mistake
> > Fancies as lost, I have stored for thee at home:
> > Rise, clasp My hand and come!'
> Halts by me that footfall:
> Is my gloom, after all,
> Shade of His hand, outstretched caressingly?
> Ah fondest, blindest, weakest,
> I am He Whom thou seekest!
> Thou dravest love from Thee, who dravest Me![8]

What do we seek? Is it a making whole of the partialness that we feel, a wholeness that can be attained by our commitment to constant striving? Is it an uneasiness to do what we have left undone, unaccomplished, or perhaps untried? These possibilities are not likely, I believe. Both suggest continued activity rather than a rest to lessen our restlessness. Rather, I believe that we seek a connection with Someone of great significance. We seek our place in that relationship. We long for the conviction that a union does indeed exist and that we are with (or in, or at least alongside) this One of greatness. It may be, as the British theologian-apologist-author C. S. Lewis suggests in "The Weight of Glory" that we long to be noticed by God. It is

> the secret we cannot hide and cannot tell, though we desire to do both. We cannot tell it because it is a desire for something that has never actually appeared in our experience. We cannot hide it because our experience is constantly suggesting it.

> . . . Physical hunger does not prove that man will
> get any bread; he may die of starvation on a raft
> in the Atlantic. But surely a man's hunger does
> prove that he comes of a race which repairs its
> body by eating and inhabits a world where eatable
> substances exist . . . Apparently, then, our lifelong
> nostalgia, our longing to be reunited with some-
> thing in the universe from which we now feel cut
> off . . . is no mere neurotic fancy, but the truest
> index of our real situation.[9]

Lewis's words might suggest to some readers that there
is an existence totally separate from this world and a life that
we must await before our restlessness is lessened. I argue that
the life, death, and resurrection of Jesus, whatever loyalty or
faith commitment we feel for that person, demonstrates a
continuity between what we now experience and what will
be experienced, for example, after death. We have explored
our ideas about time and found them to be quite arbitrary in
the sense of measurement and description; we have to face
the likelihood that our concepts of space are limited to what
our human understanding can embrace. Modern physics
has a great deal to teach us about these matters, but the
totality of what can be learned from physics does not explain,
but only conceptualizes.

What we offer here is simply that the extraordinary,
whether referring to time or space or other human concepts,
is continuous with the ordinary. For example, eternity does
not begin later for each of us but is very much now. The
mystery of ourselves as original creations reminds us that we
are just that: originals known by the divine Creator, whether
or not we can understand. In many ways, the teachings of
Jesus urge us to consider the possibility that our true being is
not self-contained, but is shared by the divine being; I
am most "myself" when I realize (discover and let be made
real) my identity in Jesus Christ. This ongoing, continuous

experience is sometimes awesomely evident and sometimes so much beyond my awareness and understanding as to seem improbable.

In any case, our challenge is not to discover who we are but rather to become aware of whose we are. We cannot possibly discover our original selves without involving our originator. Meanwhile, our busyness and our desire to remain in control obscure the necessity of our relationship with God. Some of us refuse to give up control to almost anything, only painfully and often suddenly to discover that we are being controlled by our own stress-laden compulsiveness.

6
Sabbath:
A Radical Concept Today

How may we be deeply involved in setting our own life course without falling victim to our limitations? How can we do this in the here and now, unless we find a method? The temptation is to give too easy answers to such questions, perhaps following either of two common courses. The first course is to refuse to perpetuate the crowdedness by simply saying no to continued movement and filling of our lives. A second course is to explore possibilities beyond our own resources; indeed, we might venture to explore beyond human resources, which seem often to provide only temporary relief.

I invite readers to explore an almost abandoned friend of the active life. That friend is sabbath, today largely cast in the role of a childhood acquaintance whom we have outgrown. I do not doubt that some readers will resist, asserting that sabbath was tried for centuries and didn't work. I thus beg temporary indulgence.

The word *sabbath* elicits a great variety of notions and emotions. Some people believe that sabbath is a special day in a week of seven days, while other persons concede only that the word means "seventh." To a number of people, Jewish and Christian alike, sabbath bespeaks religious and community rituals and customs. To still other persons, the word suggests an enforced change from labor to less taxing activities. (A brief look at history will reveal that there have been very wide differences of opinion about what sorts of "nonlabor" were permissible and which were to be avoided. During the period of Puritan dominance, for example, the requirements imposed upon the community were very strict on the issue of which sports were tolerable and which were not.) So many interpretations of sabbath have been championed that the word has been more or less put aside.

Early Views of Sabbath

As we probe the subject of possible spiritual responses to human stress, we can profitably explore some of the earliest concepts of sabbath. First, the equivalent Hebrew word comes from a root meaning to cease or desist: there is no implication to do. Some scholars suggest that in very early ages to do anything might have been viewed as offending one of the many gods. With the very important perception of a single God of the universe, spirituality was able to evolve in new ways. Thereafter, the opportunities and requirements for rest were viewed as God-given, and thus sacred. And since Yahweh was perceived as a God who cares for and about human beings, the people concluded that God cares about our rest—how our time of rest is "spent," we might say today.

In Genesis, Yahweh sets an example in the first mention of sabbath. In the midst of the divine busyness of creation, the Creator pauses each day to consider what has been accomplished, "and God saw that it was good!" (Gen. 1:12, e.g.). Then, at the end of the creative process, there is the seventh day of rest and reflection—daily and periodic pauses for an appreciation of the accomplishment. In the scriptural view, sabbath is the occasion when rest and restlessness intentionally meet. Subsequently, as the Bible story unfolds, there appear a variety of specific expressions of how sabbath rest will be both possible and acceptable.

The Hebrew Bible, which Christians know as the Old Testament, provides much evidence that, by about the year 1300 B.C., the Hebrews had become an empirical people, moving from a deductive to an inductive way of reasoning. The person who deals with life deductively can be viewed as having preconceptions into which she or he tries to fit daily observations, perhaps even to force a fit. The inductive approach begins with observation of the evidence at hand and proceeds to an awareness of the repeated regularity of the evidence, the generation of conclusions (such as the connection of cause and effect), and the construction of a framework by which to draw upon the discovery. The inductive method can be termed a trial-and-error approach, with the number of errors diminishing as the discoveries are repeatedly tested.

Essentially, the ancient Hebrew people explored the relationship between how life is lived and the quality of that life. I surmise that key steps in their exploration were paying attention to signs and evidence, pondering the implications of this information, perceiving a pattern within the observations, deciding upon a generalizing guideline, and being faithful in subsequent actions to the conclusion. For example, the people inhabiting a coastal area might conclude, over a period of years, that more persons became ill after eating mussels taken from the tidepools during the hotter months of summer than during any other period of the year. Wisdom would suggest that the mollusks not be eaten during the hot summer months. Moreover, the influential members of the tribe, for protection of the less observant, might prohibit consumption of mussels at all times. Perhaps in such a way did the dietary laws come into being, their gradual evolution requiring the passage of a number of human generations.

How might the requirement for sabbath rest have evolved? Again I suggest that sensitive awareness and ethical concern guided its inception. Animals that labored day after day without rest would ultimately weaken, and the range of their useful years would decrease if indeed death did not occur prematurely (e.g., Exod. 23:12). The same was recorded to be true of human slaves. For both economic and ethical reasons, ancient people eventually saw continuous and unrelieved enforced labor to be poor stewardship of resources. Significantly, sabbath rest was respected even during the strenuous planting and harvesting seasons when the need for labor increased and the risk of unfavorable weather was considered a major factor. Perhaps less evident was the need for land to rest every seventh year; vineyards and orchards lay fallow as well as fields used for annual crops (e.g., Exod. 23:10f.). This practice might have been a precursor to what colonial Americans rediscovered: the need to rotate crops on a parcel of land that we now know would otherwise be depleted of the necessary minerals and nutrients that a particular crop would extract over a period of a few years. Again, the process involved learning from subtle signs.

I suspect that one of the slowest steps in apprehending the need for sabbath was uniformity of adherence to the practice of rest. A farmer or merchant might agree on the principle of providing respite, but the requisite amount of rest might be debated. And as regarded one's own obligation to rest, there were undoubtedly persons then, as today, who would readily agree upon the principle but not on its application to themselves—as a soldier might predict that many casualties will result from a beachhead attack, but the thought may not enter his mind that he could be one of the unlucky number.

Another element bears upon our consideration of modern stress and links us to ancient peoples. There are and always have been both high-energy people and less energetic people in all periods of history. The energetic merchant of yesteryear might object to taking any time off, having decided to establish several new caravansaries, which necessitates added travel to keep abreast of local management. But tribal consensus might conclude that, at the projected rate, the merchant would soon own everything of worth, and some elders would need to have a heart-to-heart talk with him. After this experience was repeated in many subtribes by many merchants for many years with consequent envy and strife ensuing, legislated guidelines for control evolved. Tribal peace necessitated tribal concurrence on limits, including a regulated practice of rest.

We should note that the vital dimension of this imagined high-energy caravan operator allows his continued functional expressions, but his high energy comes into opposition with the sociocultural dimension. Whatever the analysis, the final product is a complex codified law, extending into far more detail than the Ten Commandments.

The Gospels tell us that Jesus repeatedly came into conflict with the legal interpretations of sabbath and consequently with the authorities who sought to enforce the whole body of law. The writer of the Gospel according to John describes how Jesus healed a man whose illness had oppressed him for thirty-eight years, then comments, "It was because Jesus did things such as this on the sabbath that they began to persecute him" (John 5:16, NAB). The continuing controversy is reported in a number of accounts and clearly arose from his breaking of sabbath (by the work done in healing on sabbath) and leading others to break sabbath rest as they came in multitudes to be healed.[1]

Jesus demonstrated that, in bringing wholeness to human beings, something greater than an adherence to law or to the observance of cultic religious worship is involved. There should be more concern for the restoration of human life than for the retrieval of a sheep from its fall into a pit, for example (Matt. 12:11). The law allowed watering an ox on the sabbath but prohibited healing a woman who had been ill for eighteen years (Luke 13:10–17). Cultic circumcision was practiced on sabbath day, but healing the whole person was not acceptable to the protectors of law (John 7:22f.).

Jesus protested, "The sabbath was made for man, not man for the sabbath" (Mark 2:27). Thus, we need to keep in mind that sabbath still has a purpose today, one that restores us in times of stress as it restored the health of persons many centuries ago.

It is easy for us to focus attention on the miraculous nature of the healings that Jesus performed and to overlook or undervalue some of the less obvious changes that took place in the lives of the persons on whom the miracles were performed (a word commonly used as if the persons were only dramatic stages on which the miracles could be demonstrated). The new movement of limbs was accompanied by joy and thankful outburst, and the first sight for eyes from which blindness had been banished was the face of God! The return of health pointed to a God who gives life and cares very much to do so. Sometimes healing was accompanied by an expressed longing for continued union with such a God. Surely there was a new treasuring of self—that self had been valued enough by a wandering rabbi that he would risk imprisonment or even death to give new life on the sabbath.

Persons whose lives were touched by such love were forever changed. More than one interpreter wrote in the ensuing centuries that the process of being loved makes us lovable, and we are able to love because we have experienced love—echoing John's letters to the early church, "We love because he [God] first loved us" (1 John 4:19). So we grasp the truth that we are valued. That valuing can arise within as well as outside of ourselves and can be kept new by a regular assessment: Which of my practices facilitate my being loved?

Jesus offered a new perspective, a new viewpoint from which to observe and value life. In broad terms, his example pointed the way to a change from a rigid legal structure to the more fluid world of relationships. The matter of perspective is very important—the proper relationship among the many elements of our lives. For example, a large structure photographed too close up seems to loom over the viewer, and the surrounding context is relativized to a secondary emphasis. Viewing a painting from a distance provides a more appropriate relationship between view and viewer. In the same way, sabbath enables us to step back from pressures that loom so large as to claim an unhealthy fraction of our awareness and concern. One gift that we can receive from regular and valued sabbath rest is new perspective. Happily, this new perspective is about life itself, especially as the different aspects of life are placed in health-giving relation to each other. Our rest can bring into balance elements that we have given excessive emphasis over other expressions of life. Locating such disproportionate emphasis might point to the sources of stress in our lives.

Gaining a New Perspective

A faithful observation of sabbath will likely provide a new perspective on life and will point out which elements are truly important in relation to other elements. Achieving such a realization might require the life-experience of living for months or years. But I encourage the reader to start the process now with a new perspective of sabbath (of any duration) gained through reflection on the following suggestions.

Intentionally break the cycle of busyness. This commitment might take the form of absenting yourself from the normal work or home environment or marking the calendar to protect your period of rest.

Rest for the purpose of seeking God's presence and not only for some useful purpose, such as girding up for next week's work.

Give a substantial fraction of an otherwise active period to rest each day, week, or month.

Dignify rest by regularity; value it as much as an equivalent period of work.

Rest with an openness for discovery, including discovery of the importance of a rhythm of activity and rest. The issue is not activity or rest, but activity and rest!

Claim rest as if it has the force of divine commandment, but do not rest simply to be compliant.

Be willing to assess whether your observance is restorative and vitalizing for body, mind, and spirit. If, after faithful observance of sabbath, you remain vague on this assessment, inquire of a wise friend how she or he perceives your state of restedness versus stressfulness.

We can draw upon thousands of years of human experience with ready-made patterns of sabbath observance. Some models are helpful, some are destructive; most are probably better than what an undisciplined person is likely to be experiencing at present.

I am reminded, as I write, of identical conversations that I had several times with a close friend who was fond of Sunday morning golf. His opening remark was sometimes a challenge, sometimes a defensive gesture, but his words were invariably, "Doug, I can worship God as well on the golf course as I can in church." For the first few exchanges, I rose to the challenge readily but not helpfully. One day, after his usual opening, I responded without thinking, "Sure you can, but do you?" Several years passed before I realized that he had been waiting for someone to question him on that point. In the same way, my suggestions about seeking a new perspective of sabbath are intended to challenge set patterns and especially to allow scrutiny of excessive busyness as illuminated by the well-tested alternative of intentional rest.

In many ways, this chapter has ranged widely over a subject about which the reader might already have a number of well-considered ideas. But despite distortions of the past and of differing views today, sabbath is indeed worthy of reconsideration by countless busy people. This consideration will best be done in the openness of an inductive/experiential perspective, rather than as a rigid preconception that is adhered to mindlessly. I further suggest that present avoidance of sabbath rest arises not from a sense that such rest is unhelpful, but because the idea of sabbath challenges our presupposed values regarding acquisition of wealth or personal power in the workplace.

The Radical Nature of Sabbath

Sabbath rest is a very radical concept, and our fidelity to its observances will require a substantial measure of commitment for several reasons. First of all, the idea of simple rest is countercultural. (This point has been discussed earlier in connection with modern notions of time.) We are all aware that official national and state holidays ensure periodic freedom from usual work schedules. Three-day weekends are frequently periods of intense movement, however, and are scarcely restful. Recreational facilities form an important element of a major industry (sometimes complete with recreation directors!), but basic rest is the focus for few of these offerings.

The second reason that sabbath is a radical concept comes from the connection between the commandment to keep the sabbath holy and the shaping of society. (Certainly, acceptance of that commandment came only after greatly differing viewpoints had interacted.) The Old Testament tells about Amos, one of the earliest prophets (eighth century B.C.), who accuses the merchants of wanting the sabbath to pass so that they can resume their dishonest practices (Amos 8:5). Jeremiah, two centuries later, reveals that the prohibition against carrying burdens on the sabbath is connected with the desire to enter the gates of Jerusalem, where ready buyers might be available (Jer. 17:21f.). Still later, Nehemiah (about 450 B.C.) reports the breaking of sabbath observance for harvest, and he condemns men of Tyre for selling fish and all kinds of wares to the people of Judah and in Jerusalem (Neh. 13:15–22). Imagine the upset of local merchants! Throughout sabbath observance is a reminder that persons in power must deal justly with the powerless, a major ethical decision about sabbath rest for all: "Remember that you too were once slaves in Egypt" (Deut. 5:15, NAB). The strict observance of sabbath strongly affected the shaping of society; probably only the first commandment ("You shall have no other gods but me") was more influential in forming a nation and a religious heritage.

I suggest that a similar valuing of rest can continue to shape individuals and nations today; at a societal level, a uniform practice of rest would bring opposite viewpoints into open conflict. Modern opinions differ widely regarding whether the material is more valued than the personal. Some believe that both individual values and civil legal codes give priority to the material. In any case, the one who rests while others work experiences some level of disapproval. Regular sabbath rest is indeed resisted! One who rests regularly must anticipate disapproval from an active society!

A third indication of sabbath's radical nature is its testing of our belief in divine grace, whether God will indeed provide or whether each of us needs to be in charge of a disproportionate fraction of the universe. Not to be open to rest is to deny the deep presence of God in our lives. I have been both participant and listener in theological discussions of the justification issue that St. Paul raises in the New Testament (Rom. 3, 4, e.g.). A basic question arises: What is required that God will consider us acceptable? St. Paul and countless theologians (and others not so trained) argue that it is not by works that we are justified, but by faith—our faith in God and faithfulness to God's expectations for us (or by God's faithfulness to us, some would prefer). Truth to tell, however, we live much of our lives as if what we do will make possible the relationship with God that we desire, while we think and profess that the gift comes through faith. Rest, then, is radical because it calls upon us to live what we profess: God provides, and God loves us as we are.

Fourth, as the word radical (from Latin *radix*, meaning root) suggests, sabbath rest makes possible the deepest nurturing we can know. In short, such rest gets right to the root of the matter to correct our body's overdoing.

Rabbi Abraham Heschel, a theologian, mystic, and social reformer during the middle of this century, gave a clue to the place of sabbath in the modern world.

> On the Sabbath we try to become attuned to holiness in time. It is a day on which we are called upon to share in what is eternal in time, to turn from the results of creation to the mystery of creation; from the world of creation to the creation of the world.[2]

This discussion about sabbath points to the way in which the whole person, not only the body, responds to stressful life. We have noted that the parasympathetic nervous system does not prevent the action of the sympathetic nervous system, but functions parallel to and after it in a restorative, complementary way. Sabbath serves a similar purpose in an active life and, like the parasympathetic nervous system, brings its quieting gifts unbidden.

7

Reflection:
Awareness of God's Assistance

Where and how can we encounter the wonders of creation so that we can marvel about them? Ample material for wonder is offered in the midst of daily experiences, though this primary source might often be undervalued or even overlooked. Poet Walt Whitman wrote:

> Why should I wish to see God better than this day?
> I see something of God each hour of the twenty-
> four, and each moment then;
> In the faces of men and women I see God, and in
> my own face in the glass;
> I find letters from God drop't in the street—and
> every one is sign'd by God's name,
> And I leave them where they are, for I know that
> wheresoe'er I go,
> Others will punctually come forever and ever.[1]

The *where* is in daily life; if we are able to reclaim life incidents as basic data for wonder, the issue then becomes *when* and *how* this rich information can be deeply appropriated. What a loss it would be for us if wonder were confined to one day per week, when the freshness of an experience might not remain! Thus, the fullness of sabbath should be experienced at least daily, perhaps more frequently. Such observance of sabbath (*observance* meaning celebration) can be tied in with our deepened awareness of life (i.e., observing or paying attention to life). In this chapter I shall discuss the practice of reflection on everyday experiences, on incidents that occur frequently and that might go unappreciated were we not to call them back to awareness. Such reflection can become the *how* of daily sabbath and thereby the foundation for an ongoing spiritual response to life's pressures.[2]

The frequent sabbaths that I recommend involve breaking the cycle of our busyness, then consciously putting aside what is planned for later in the day, relinquishing all expectations of some payoff, and restfully reconsidering some event that comes to our awareness from our routine of the past few days. This respite for reflection allows gentle recollection of what has already been given in life. There are other opportunities to think about current events or history or concepts; this intentional sabbath is periodic quiet for the purpose of thoughtfully pondering our own lives.

Mary, the mother of Jesus, is the central figure in two examples of personal reflection. The first event is the visitation of the shepherds to the birth scene in Bethlehem (Luke 2:6–20). The shepherds seem to burst into the stable, where they tell Mary and the others of a startling encounter with an angelic choir that has appeared to them in the fields. We can imagine only part of the thoughts that must have passed through Mary's mind, not the least startling of which would have been that men from one of the lowest strata of society were the ones to whom the angels appeared. The words of these simple shepherds confirm what the angel Gabriel had announced to Mary nine months before, not only about a future birth, but about the very special nature of the child. What did Mary do? She pondered the matter, some Bibles inform us; another version records, "Mary kept all these things, pondering them in her heart" (Luke 2:19, RSB). The New English Bible expresses that Mary "treasured up," as if the product of her reflection added to a store of preciousness to assure that the treasure not be lost.[3] In the same way, our reflection can often lessen the pressure for further acquisition when we perceive how much treasure we already have.

The second example of Mary's reflection should elicit a sympathetic response from parents of adolescent children. This account is found in Luke 2:41–52. The event follows a visit by many holiday pilgrims to the holy city of Jerusalem at the time of the Passover feast. Mary and Joseph are among a number of families on their three-day return trip to Galilee. Jesus' parents are aware only at day's end that the boy is not with the band traveling together. We hardly need pause to imagine the mixture of concern, anger, and embarrassment that the parents feel when it becomes clear that their lad is not with the group of other children.

We can relate to the feelings of the parents who must await daylight before returning to Jerusalem—and imagine the wildness and dangers that they experience in the crowded city. After three anxious days, the parents reconnect with the boy. They are confronted with words that will prove to be prophetic, but that, at the time, must have been irritating: "Why do you search for me? Did you not know that I had to be in my Father's house?" For our discussion, the pertinent detail is Mary's response. She pondered the matter and somehow was able to let it enrich her life, as again she treasured what life had offered.

In both instances, Mary dealt with very stressful events reflectively. She did not repress that which she could not quickly explain or even appropriate. She apparently let go of the experiences in some way, allowing what was in her mind and heart to remain partially unresolved. Therein, Mary exemplifies our process of reflecting on life. She did not confine the incidents within her ongoing self-examination (introspection) but "handed back" her memories, feelings, and state of mind while they were current as, for example, a mirror gives back an image of the viewer. Transcendent reflection, then, is not limited to a rethinking or even pondering or marveling, but also includes a handing back.[4]

One time-honored way to "hand back" is to offer a personal matter in prayer, whatever its details. If the experience is positive, the loveliness may abound all the more in sharing it; if negative or painful, the burden may be lightened. Note that such sharing in prayerful release, whether in joyful thanksgiving or in burdened petition for divine support, assures that reflection will not be limited to a method, but will involve relationship with God. Intellectual analysis does not constitute deep reflection of the sort being discussed; our intellects must be penetrated by wonder and awe if the lessons of life are to be "treasured up" in our hearts!

A Simple Guide for Transcendent Reflection

Practical guidelines are useful, whether to apply these assistances to our lives or to seek only to understand what is written on these pages. There is no single way to reflect upon life's offerings, but the following elements are necessarily involved.

> An incident occurs prereflectively. In other words, life happens.

> Somewhat later, we consciously bring details of the incident back in our memory, under circumstances as free from distraction as possible. However, if the setting is not so peaceful as we might prefer, it is better to give the incident whatever attention we can rather than to postpone the attempt and thus perhaps not to reflect about life at all.

Some recalled element might warm our hearts, or make a connection with earlier wonderings, or repeatedly come to mind. Thereupon, we let ourselves be captured by that lead, then gently and restfully listen with our hearts to whatever insights we receive. Though it might sound flippant, we allow ourselves to flow with the incident that claims our presence and attention.

In due course, we might inquire, What does this incident tell me about my life? or Does this experience suggest that I might alter my views or actions in life?

We intentionally release all that has occurred to God. The prayerful release might take the form: Thank you, Lord, for the new insight. Or it could be: God, I've wrestled with this as much as I care to; you may have it all.

If, right at this instant, I should begin to rewrite the preceding paragraph, it might turn out quite differently, for there is no limit to the number of ways in which one can pray, or daydream, or think reflectively. I hope that this will encourage the reader to test and experiment with the content of what I offer, rather than to await a perfect or even proper method of reflection.

A major point should be noted about the purpose of intentional reflection: life is not to be simply passed through without occasionally being evaluated. Thus, one outcome of the reflection is that the individual has purposely devoted time and attention to valuing her or his life. Socrates is said to have remarked that the unexamined life is not worth living. That is, indeed, a hard saying! But I do believe that an examined life is more treasured than a life not reflected upon; I daresay that life is enriched in the process. Volumes have been written about the spiritual life; however else the spiritual life can be described, it is a reflective life.

An examined life surely suggests to the reader an element of critical and incisive appraisal, for we recall the moments of uneasiness before school examinations, physical examinations, or interviews for employment. I suggest that we add a gentleness to our reflections, a kindliness to ourselves. If we allow the reflection to proceed quietly, we shall gently put aside the pressures. If, on the other hand, we are calculative, we will probably not be gentle, but will continue to experience stress as we seek a payoff. We can be honest without being cuttingly analytical; indeed, we shall more likely continue to allow ourselves to be reflective if we are honest and gentle. Without self-honesty, we might simply admire an image of ourselves and not come to treasure the self we know is not perfect. In being gentle, we deal with ourselves as we would with anything else that is vulnerable and precious, such as a tiny infant child, a small kitten, or a delicate work of sculpture. Imagine that Mary of Nazareth dealt with the experiences of her life in a gentle manner, retaining them in the center of her being—as suggested by the word *heart* as the focus of her treasuring.

Formation through Reflection

Though we do not set out to ask that reflection produce some profitable output, spiritual growth is a frequent outcome. Prayerful reflection tells us about the persons we are and the persons we are becoming. In other words, reflection informs us about our ongoing spiritual formation. I offer an illustration from my own life. The setting is the common room of a retreat center where I had gone for a weekend conference. As I sensed within myself a mixture of a desire to be with other people and yet to be uninvolved, I sat in the corner of the large lounge area where, unrealistically, I hoped that both wishes could be met. After I had enjoyed relative silence for much of an hour, other retreatants began to arrive and the sound level increased. The major sounds were those of people greeting each other, and I classified the animated sound of many conversations as noise. In the meantime, a young monk sat at a piano opposite my corner of the room and began to play skillfully and rather quietly. Though the overall sound level rose considerably, I rated the music as a pleasant sound, not noise, and I strained to hear it. A young woman moved to stand near the piano. I hastily judged her move to be flirtatious, judged her so, and thereupon forgot the musical offering.

I found myself reflecting about this incident some hours later and on other occasions during the next few years (and again now, some fifteen years still later!). I have realized that the way in which I responded was most informative about myself, and that my new insight was possible only because I intentionally brought the matter back to mind. My judgments of others' motives—horror of horrors—can be self-righteous, for example! Furthermore, I sometimes want to have my cake and eat it too in my unreasonable effort to be both in and apart from a group. An even more painful realization, endured for thirty years prior to that experience, was the admission that I not only regret but also resent my lack of musical ability, a thought of which I was not aware while in the common room.

Reviewing my example, reflection often unfolds as follows: an incident; some unreflective spontaneous response on my part; reflection, with a growing self-awareness; and self-affirmation—for example, that it is all right not to be a musician. As I relive the incident, I realize that I shall never be a performer but I am blessed to enjoy music. Moreover, I no longer need to explain my lack of musical ability or to feel the old pain of being put down by a music teacher in my junior high school days! Reviewing the experience from the beginning, I realize that a continuing treasure is revealed to me as I continue to respond to my spontaneous response to a quite ordinary occurrence years earlier.

Modifying How We Respond

From one viewpoint, to act impulsively and freely is to be myself—the person who acts out of dispositions, rather than one who responds solely to stimuli or to restraints imposed externally. Thus the actions that we express prereflectively are a valuable source of information about ourselves. Our gentle reflection on events can make us deeply aware of how we interface with other persons and with the natural world, as well as the extent to which the way we live conforms to our philosophical views. Moreover, this incident-response rhythm allows us to confirm a present natural response to certain types of circumstances. For example, we might strengthen the way in which we are learning to respond patiently, rather than always rushing toward a quick resolution in conversation with another person.

What is this dispositional response to incidents in our daily life? I believe we act (or respond or react) in rather typical ways because those actions require an expenditure of minimum energy on our part. That is to say, we don't need to stop at each new situation in order to mentally explore all of the options and then to select one as our mode of response. Instead, we almost automatically act in the mode with which we are comfortable due to many previous testings. Those previous incidents would have been accompanied by decisions and our living with the consequences of the decisions. For example, one person might have concluded decades earlier that he would never again undergo a deprivation of physical comfort as he had experienced in childhood and will consistently seek to drive a hard bargain. This person might ultimately be ruled by a disposition of hardness.

Another person might have been so captivated by student politics that she continues to look for motivation behind anyone's stated preferences and is characterized by suspicion (among her other dispositions). A third person might experience both of these outlooks as alien to her view of life and will virtually always accept a situation at face value, knowing that she can modify her level of acceptance later. Likely, she would be viewed as having a trusting disposition.[5] Note that the three persons follow a nonexertive initial course, even if subsequent thought might lead to a desire for another sort of "automatic" response and a decision to move in a new direction. After many attempts, a new disposition could emerge.

In the process of living, we are in a state of continual change; not to change is not to be alive. After some occurrence that we follow by reflection, we are different persons. If we have decided (at whatever level of consciousness) that we accept the way we responded to the event, we become more confirmed in that response. On the other hand, we may have decided (irrespective of the level of consciousness) to seek to change our response. Again, we are different persons after the event. Note that these changes are often so slight as to be undetectable at the moment and only become detectable in hindsight some days or months later.

Thus, personal growth or ongoing formation occurs in a cyclic movement. Again, the general elements involve something "just happening," then our immediate response, subsequent recollection and reflection, a conclusion and perhaps a decision that will directly affect future encounters of this sort when they "just happen." The combination of elements is not adequately described as linear, for we do not move continuously and directly from a starting point to a destination. Nor can we describe the sequence as following a circular path. Although we might return to almost the same point where we were prior to the encounter, our disposition has moved forward or backward: more or less hard, wary, or trusting in our three examples. Our progress, then, seems to follow the course of a helix; that is, traversing a near-circular course for each cycle and proceeding in a linear direction. (The configuration of wire in a coil spring is a physical example.) After any given incident, we move briefly in either direction, but after a long period and many incidents, the linear movement is forward or backward, depending on our decisions and commitments.

After many experiences and many periods of reflection, we take on more of a disposition, for example, patience, so that in subsequent incidents we are more likely to respond in patience without prior reflection. When we tend to respond in patience, we are predisposed to act patiently. The changed person with a patient disposition acts patiently with a minimum expenditure of energy in a pressure-loaded situation. We have, by testing our choices many times, been deeply and personally involved in our formation. This is quite different from being shaped only by pressures, as the copper sheets in shop class were completely shaped by blows from hammers!

The Importance of Release

By no means do I suggest that the reflection process is simply that of introspective analysis. There also needs, very much, to be the element of handing back, of transcendence, of going beyond ourselves. Perhaps reflection on painful experiences leads us most easily to a willingness to move beyond analysis to release. Consider the example of having lost a dear friend or spouse by death. All who have experienced such separation know that countless feelings and questions arise. Was I protective enough? Was I, perhaps, too protective? Did I share the really important matters with him? Was I too frank with her? The list is never-ending, and the questioning of self could go on for years. But even if acceptable answers are found for the many, many questions, only the pieces of a relationship may remain. Perhaps the relationship could now be better understood than formerly—were it not for the fact that it has been dissected! Thus we see the importance of reflecting deeply and then releasing—not releasing without reflecting, nor reflecting without releasing.

So, I suggest a helpful guideline for reflection about life events and burdens. Inquire during such meditative moments along two lines: first, whether you did or could have sensed the presence of God during your immediate response to a life event; and second, whether you are inviting God's presence while in the process of your later reflection about the event. Most likely, the second guideline can be followed by most of us, for we can intentionally prepare for reflection by quieting ourselves, choosing a time when we do not feel rushed and otherwise under constraints of self-imposed pressure. But we shall probably need to program this special time in which we can dispose ourselves to reflection.

Reflection on everyday incidents is, of course, celebrating sabbath frequently. And in so doing, we combine the two sorts of time that appear in the New Testament record. We suspend chronos and on occasion discover kairos in the here and now. Perhaps we can discover a new fullness that transcends clock time by setting aside time and sharing the outcome (or impasse) with God who is both beyond and within time.

8
Gentle Presence to Ourselves

The importance of gentleness in reflection was brought to my attention several years ago as I thought about paintings I had recently seen at an art exhibit. While in the museum, my thoughts were at times negatively critical. Subsequent quiet rumination about my pickiness gave me insights on the nature of human originality; I was able to receive the insights because I had reserved comment and did not thereby dismiss the subject without thoughtful consideration.

To be candid, my tongue was checked only for fear that I would diminish some of my wife's excitement as she stood before a number of paintings on special exhibit. I did, however, comment at the time, "Look, Picasso has managed to draw a picture of Madonna and Child in only fifteen or so lines!" (Only later did I realize that the gift of artistic genius had captured the expression of maternal love with so few brush strokes.) Some minutes prior to this comment, I had stood close before an impressionistic painting by Cézanne, observing silently that it was really nothing more than an assemblage of many brush-daubed dots of various pastel colors. But when I stood at a distance from the canvas, the scene took shape and invited my imagination to personalize and appreciate a fine work of art. The dots of paint allowed me to forgo comparison between the painting and my tastes and to accept an object of art without its first having passed the judgment of my preconceptions.

My reflections continued and insights followed. I realized that the two works could not be compared with each other, nor with other paintings that had caught my attention earlier. Originals defy comparison. What one needs to do in a confrontation with an original—painting or person—is not to be involved in comparison, but in compassion. One "feels with," as the word compassion suggests; one can be present to the mystery without being expected to change or fix or even understand.

How affirming it is to experience that another person is fully present to us! How assuringly the presence of the other steadies us in moments of uncertainty! Sometimes that presence is expressed by silence, sometimes by the other person simply listening to us. Their affirmation proclaims with the German philosopher Josef Pieper, "It's good that you exist!"[1] The recipient of such presence does not hear the message, It's good that you exist because of what you have accomplished, but perceives simply a rejoicing in the existence of one of God's original creations.

We have all experienced these affirming encounters in our lives, and thus we know firsthand the power of presence. Alternatively, we might painfully recall a feeling of rejection when the other person innocently glanced at a clock while we were sharing most deeply or assured us prematurely out of her own anxiety that everything would be all right, when we so deeply felt that life would never be the same again!

The same dynamic affirmation is implicit in the practice of quiet solitary reflection. Often, it is difficult for us to accept affirmation from ourselves. I have suggested earlier that a disciplined life carries with it the gift of self-affirmation—we can consider ourselves valuable enough to provide healthy self-care. When we dedicate a significant effort to disciplined reflection without demanding an immediate reward, we discover later that our practice has nurtured ourselves—an important effort for the well-being of a person to whom we have begun to give new value. In this way, our valuing of self grows. I am not describing arrogant self-importance, but a valuing in the way that God and other loving persons value us.We become self-valuing when another person values our presence.

If we maintain written journals, for example, we record our spiritual ruminations because that discipline helps us to sense our spiritual well-being, as truly as fidelity to regular medical examinations apprises us of the state of our physical health. So also with daily attentiveness to the body's rejoicing in being alive even as it maintains itself through physical exercise. With fair regularity, I have been a jogger for more than a decade. On most occasions, I approach the first steps with a mixture of thoughts. Early in a morning's run, I might ask myself, Why are you doing this? You know you don't like it! Then, after running for about three fourths of a mile, I realize that my resistance has changed to acceptance, and I enjoy the sensation of movement and of the coordination of muscles as well as the roadside sights. After running and preparing for the day's work, there remains just beyond my awareness what has been called "formative memory," a residue from the experience, which will encourage me to a similar exertion next time.[2]

Examining Our Awareness in the Present

I have discussed the recollection of and reflection on past life events. A similar fidelity to awareness can help us to reflect on the present and to offer back to God what is even now taking place. If we are oriented to an efficient use of time (whatever that might mean), we might be inclined to reflect after the fact, if at all. But to be attentive in the midst of busy activity is to offer to God the precious element of time that escapes our control. To give of the present is like the giving of life, which is also passing. I hope that this possibility will become more evident and acceptable as this chapter proceeds, but I strongly suspect that real agreement can come only out of regular and prolonged personal experience and practice.

The Ignatian Exercises,[3] which the Jesuits have so well developed, contain a carefully outlined set of guidelines for the examination of conscience.[4] In one format of a thirty-day retreat, for example, a director assists a retreatant in a week-long examination of conscience. The following procedure might be used to examine a personal defect three times each day. Upon arising, retreatants resolve to guard against a particular sin or defect that they wish to correct. Later, after noon and evening meals, they prayerfully seek to recall how many times they have fallen victim to the sin or defect and mark a chart for each occurrence. This hour-by-hour chart can then be used to show for a particular day or week how the defect has been amended. I view the process as too highly structured for my ready acceptance, although I know that it has been helpful for other people.

While I do not follow the written method suggested in the *Exercises*, I have found it very important to pause regularly and to inquire about my attentiveness to my inner life. Most days I find myself in late morning automatically inquiring mentally about the nature of the day thus far. My inquiry is in general terms: How has the morning gone, Doug? How would you like the afternoon to go? My inquiry is certainly brief and simple, but the questions speak directly to my day's activities, to the way in which I am spending and directing my life. Usually, I also inquire, Where has God been in your morning, Doug? and How would you like God to be involved in your afternoon? I have found these questions more helpful in dealing with daily pressures than aspirin or antacid tablets when noon comes!

I have realized that my inquiries are not so much an examination of conscience as an examination of consciousness, or awareness of God's presence. Mainly, however, the process uncovers the intensity of my busyness, often at the cost of losing my sense of perspective. Such intensity can foster productivity at the expense of other persons or tasks that need my presence.

Therein lies a wealth of material for my continued contemplation: questions of constant movement versus fixity, the risk of running through life versus the dread of finding myself in a rut. I have already confessed my decades-long pattern of wanting to remain in motion, which in later years I acknowledge as an expression of a search for my place in the universe. Moreover, my tendency was fostered early in professional life by the clear message from two corporations for which I worked: An employee must keep moving, not only to get ahead but to avoid being left behind. How this encouraged my unfolding suspicion that I might actually be indispensable! This viewpoint is also expressed in the messianism that afflicts a good fraction of clergy and other "people helpers." Alas, this mild desire to change the world single-handedly is but one origin of workaholism and professional burnout.

Constant activity does not foster the practice of presence to others, nor to the lilies of the field, nor to our own lives. On the other hand, our preconceptions might suggest that decreased activity indicates a disregard for the larger context. We fear that we shall become embedded in life if we do not stay in motion. Thus, to live between these extremes, it seems imperative to be aware of life and to accept it as it is.

Presence to Our Own Life Settings

Perhaps the admission that our lives are situated in time and space is the best starting point in seeing life as it is: by the century in which we are born, by the continent or country in which we live, by our sex, by our station in life, and by other external factors. We can view these circumstances as oppressively restrictive, and therefore negative. Or, we can see the same circumstances as very liberating. In that light, the limitations are positive—I no longer have a compulsion to be in charge of the universe. I am freed from the infinite number of choices that urge me first in one direction and then in several others. As this realization is accepted willingly, we can "bloom where we are planted," in the words of a slogan that was popular a decade or so ago.

The Benedictine vow of monastic stability provides a helpful insight to nonmonastics about the binding and freeing aspects of where we are situated. In professing this vow, the monk or sister promises to remain in the same physical setting for life, except when a group from the community relocates together. Such a promise is startling to our highly mobile society. "What!" many might exclaim, "Do you mean to say that you are promising to live out the rest of your life on these thirty acres with twenty-four others of the religious community? You must be out of your mind!" But their vow of stability illustrates a belief that, if God is not to be met on those thirty acres, who is to say that God is to be found anywhere?

And on the issue of our place in time (whether by century or age), who is to say that God is to be encountered at any other time, past or future, if God is not to be encountered also in the present—not just these present years but in each present moment? Jesus said, somewhat to the consternation of the calculating, controlling side of each of us, "Enough, then, of worrying about tomorrow. Let tomorrow take care of itself" (Matt. 6:34, NAB). This thought is tersely expressed by Alcoholics Anonymous: "One day at a time."

Note that neither Jesus nor Alcoholics Anonymous recommends procrastination or lack of planning. Nor does their advice reject the treasures of the past. Rather, they suggest living more fully in the present. One way to do this is to be reflective in the present, perhaps offering the meditative experience to God. At a sports event, for example, we can allow ourselves to enjoy the present excitement without worrying about the possible heavy traffic during the homeward journey. At the start of a meal, we can savor the awareness of what a gift an appetite is while we enjoy the food. At Fourth of July fireworks, the excitement of the crowd can be valued along with the colorful display. And in an intimate moment with another person, it is really not possible to separate my contributions from those of my loved one.

This practice of presence requires as much faithfulness as the discipline of jogging or journaling. Fortunately, we are not required to create the necessary dynamics that will allow God's presence to us. Basil Hume, the present Cardinal Archbishop of Westminster, has commented about prayer in words that provide a good analogy for journaling, jogging, or prayerful reflection: "I think that it is a truism of prayer that the desire for it follows from the practice of it."[5] So it will be in the practice of being present to ourselves as well as to the environment.

Presence to Simple Objects

Consider how we can practice being present to the world. Let us examine being present to simple objects, to scripture, to other people, and to ourselves. Imagine that you are walking slowly, intentionally aware of your environment. You are attracted to an object, perhaps a water-worn stone at the beach, a single rosebud in a garden, or a large piece of bark alongside a forest path. You take the object in your hand and gently examine it, aware of its color, texture, weight, odor, structure, and other special characteristics. You note whether it is compact and well shaped (the stone), enfolded and still living (the rosebud), or perhaps irregular and composed largely of air cells (the bark). You wonder about its origin and history. How did it happen to be where it is? You become aware of its relative simplicity (the stone) or its great intricacy (the rosebud). If you are simply present to the object, you will not use it only as a means to do something. For example, you will gently avoid pursuing such thoughts as, I must remember this morning to send some flowers to Eloise. Nor do you cut the bud from the bush to pursue an investigation of how the tightly enfolded petals can open to form a much larger flower. Instead of seeking something informative (lest the walk later be assessed as having wasted time), you remain open to what the object may say to you. "I am turned in on myself, but there is the promise of my being more open," the rose may tell you. Whatever does or does not happen, being present to a simple object can lift us from the world of busyness and stress to a childlike appreciation of the world and of the Creator who has made both world and appreciation possible.

Presence to Holy Scripture

There are many reasons for reading Holy Scripture. College students may enroll for academic credit in a class entitled "The Bible as Literature" or "The Bible as History." Some persons may read alone or in groups because of curiosity or the vague suspicion that all cultured persons should be familiar with the book that has been so important to Western culture. A major difference among our various approaches to the Scriptures lies in the fact that some of us read the Bible for the same reason that we read other books, namely because we want to know the contents, but many people read the Bible because they already know the contents quite well and have recognized the importance of being personally present to these special writings. These readers have discovered what others have perceived about the simplicity of nature: If one is open to the presence of God in either a holy book or redwood bark, God's presence will far more likely be experienced than if one is closed to the possibility.

How, then, can we be present to Holy Scripture? Although there are countless ways, I will describe only one. First, follow the urge that leads you to reread a short section, a sentence, or even a few words. Imagine that you are reading the sixth chapter of the Book of Mark. You have just read about twelve of Jesus' friends returning to him after a series of experiences in which they have discovered their own spiritual empowerment in the stressful context of public and political violence. Jesus says to them, "Come away by yourselves to a lonely place, and rest a while" (Mark 6:31, RSB). In being present to that verse and still imagining, we reread the words in our own quietness. We might imagine their physical setting in that ancient period. We might wonder why Jesus suggested rest rather than discussion. A host of other thoughts arise as we seek to put ourselves in the place of the twelve. But to be present to the reading, we also need to ask: What is being offered to me? What does this advice convey to me in my setting? Am I simply to read this as an old story? Is Jesus concerned about my needs as well as those of his twelve close friends?

Presence to Other People

As we continue to read the New Testament, we discover the inescapable message that Jesus is found in other persons. If we are to be present to the Lord who still cares for us, if we perceive him as more than as the Lord of history about whom fascinating stories were written, we must be present to other people—all sorts of people whose paths cross ours daily.

Obviously, there are more ways to be present to others than there are other people. What is one way to be present to persons? I began this chapter with the assertion that to be present to another person is to affirm that person. So, then, we need to let others share their lives with us, in the beginning perhaps most directly by simply telling parts of their stories, or whatever elements of their lives they want to share. In those moments we are attentive listeners, not constantly interrupting nor eager to talk about ourselves. Instead, we are quiet presences, not totally mute, but responding in ways that reinforce and nurture the other person who tells us one of the world's most important stories—that of a largely unknown original.

Not only can we be objectively aware of the inanimate rosebud or be present to scripture or to other persons, but we can also increase our awareness of ourselves. We can be present to ourselves. We have considered how to establish a restful setting in which reflection is possible. For me, reflection is easiest when I am alone. But often in group settings, I find that my outward appearance of involvement or non-involvement is strongly dependent on dynamics not solely under my control. Inwardly, I might ask myself how I feel when what someone expresses begins to sound critical of something or someone I hold dear. I might then decide whether to offer some defensive information immediately or to let the conversation proceed. In any case, I sense arousal within myself and the call to fight an opposing view, complete with quickening of my heartbeat. In some circumstances, notably with a dominant person, I might instead react by withdrawing my attentiveness—a simple form of flight.

In addition to whatever takes place in the group, I am also aware of what is taking place within myself. Later I might realize that I did not have to change or "fix" the person who expressed views differing from mine, nor was I called upon to understand those views fully. This realization is especially helpful when I consider other situations that are more painful than the imaginary group encounter. In experiencing presence to ourselves, we can realize, for example, that we do not need to control psychic or physical pain (by chemical or other means) the moment we become aware of that pain; nor do we need to take flight in denial, busyness, or other responses that cut short our presence to life's important messages, painful though they often are.

These examples suggest not only that I be present to persons and things in the events of my life, but that my presence involve entering the situation with an initial moderation, rather than being totally subject to the feelings of burden or threat that typify attack or retreat. An attentive person often brings something special to a situation through gentleness, even when not consciously aware of her or his own presence in that way. Such an approach is, of course, quite unacceptable to other persons who prefer always to act decisively and early. The less rushed persons might allow growth to take place as needed and then to prune, whereas the one who moves precipitously and maintains control may, in fact, prevent natural growth.

The book *Zorba the Greek* contains a touching scene in which the aspiring writer becomes aware of his surroundings in new ways. In his eagerness to witness the emergence of a butterfly from its cocoon, he breathes on the encased insect only to discover that his haste has forced an unfolding that cannot be completed, and the butterfly dies. The natural unfolding could have taken place at its own pace by the slower warming of the sun. At the sad end of his intervention, he writes: "Now it was too late. My breath had forced the butterfly to appear, all crumpled before its time."[6]

Do our responses to imperfect situations (the incidents of life!) arise from dispositions deep within us or from feelings that hover very close to the surface, vigilant for threat or opportunity? John A. T. Robinson, the late Anglican Bishop of Woolwich, succinctly reminds us of the differences between the centers and edges of the human psyche. We are often intent upon building and maintaining hard boundaries of self while not attending to our centers. He asserts that we need soft, fluid, receptive boundaries that allow our lives to merge with others while having strong centers in which Christ is very much present and gently participating in our response to situations that seem at first more than we can handle.[7] With such a divine presence, we need not resort so quickly to fight or flight; the pressures become not only bearable, but actually serve as sources of continued healthy growth. We are indeed created in the image of God. In the process of living, we become who we originally were, as our true identity is discovered in Jesus.

You might wonder whether these paragraphs are merely soft words without strong centers. I certainly hope not. But is your highly developed rational side asking for some stronger proof? Such discovery of the fullness of our true presence in the world must, of course, take place very personally in each life. I am convinced that what begins as an earnest inquiry into the present will prove to be a foretaste, the promise of ongoingness. The savoring of present vitality will be accompanied by the expectancy of future life. Why, you may ask, might this be so? Each of us experiences vitality and expectancy in sensing that we are at the beginning of an important new friendship, both with ourselves and with the Lord.

9
The Sacrament of the Everyday

I have avoided suggesting methods for defusing life's pressures so that they cease to produce the stress reaction. Instead, I have advocated that a spiritually aware person can deal with pressures in ways that are generally less stress-producing than can the person who does not value the spiritual dimensions. These suggestions arise from my own experience and from the comments of many people who have shared their spiritual journeys with me.

In writing about my viewpoint, I feel some discomfort, for from deep within me come whispers prompted by my years of research in the physical sciences wherein proofs are expected to be evident or directly measurable. However, I also believe that to ignore so much evidence breaks faith with the wisdom of science. We should be responsive to the data and insights that are given or discovered and then seek to test the initial information by a method appropriate to that area of inquiry. In the area of spiritual formation, the data and insights have come from the lives of many people.[1] Often, their experiences are consonant with the testimony of early history as recorded in Holy Scriptures and validated by the writings of the early Christian spiritual masters. The methodology (if such a word is acceptable in discussing spiritual matters) is to view the data and insights from the past of others that confirm our own past and present as not merely a matter of information but of ongoing human formation as well. The most appropriate measure for the method's efficacy is to examine the quality of life and to determine whether it is being changed for the better.

Spiritual formation is a type of growth, and, like any sort of growth, its details are mysterious. Experience helps us to understand that physical growth requires the consumption of food. Increase in size is evident in a child, while maintenance of health is the more common sign in adults. Our spiritual food is not so evident, nor is spiritual growth or ongoing nurture and maintenance of our spiritual needs. Mystery pertains to that which has already been experienced as well as that which has not yet been explored. God's gifts seem all the more mysterious when we realize that the effects are out of proportion to the effort involved. There is the element of surprise that this should be so, as if much is being created out of little or the totally unexpected has occurred. We commonly have the feeling that we have not earned or deserved God's gifts. To further complicate the matter, their unfolding is not always gradual and sequential but may include elements of the unexpected and of otherness such as is experienced in a personal relationship! In short, fullness and mystery in life cannot be proven to the satisfaction of skeptics but can, nonetheless, be experienced.

This sounds suspiciously like the church's teachings on the meaning of grace and sacraments. Without resorting to technical descriptions drawn from catechisms, and forgoing formal theological concepts, I note some of the features of sacraments that have been developed in the preceding chapters.

Everyday experiences contain the same element of the evident: that which can be seen, heard, or otherwise sensed.

Another element not perceivable through the five senses comes as a new insight and seems to break through from outside of our just-previous awareness, as if from a depth within ourselves about which we might not have been aware for some time.

There is awareness that something is being given, whether it is rest, vitality, or the sense of a new possibility for or dimension in life.

There is an unknownness or mystery about the source of the gift and, indeed, about whether the gift has come to the intended recipient. (But I have done nothing to deserve this nice surprise!)

A sense of connectedness emerges between what has been observed consciously and what has been bestowed, whether or not our reflection is perceived to make a connection between the evident and the mysterious.

A promise is acknowledged that more is to come, not as something to which we are entitled, but about which we become expectant nonetheless.

The preceding elements are drawn from my own experience. However, I arranged them in the same order as they appear in a classic statement given in the Anglican Book of Common Prayer.

Sacrament: an outward and visible sign of an inward and spiritual grace given to us, ordained by Christ himself, as a means whereby we receive the same, and a pledge to assure us thereof.[2]

Though the church (in the universal sense of all times and places) has vested a central emphasis on sacraments, there has by no means been agreement about what is meant by the word *sacrament*. There is general concurrence that the rites of Baptism and Holy Communion are the major sacraments of the church (though preferred descriptive names may vary). At various times in history, an additional five, sometimes called "sacramental acts," have been considered: confirmation (of mature commitment), ordination, matrimony, penance, and anointing of the sick. I believe that this unresolved question about what constitutes a sacrament illustrates the operation of an important principle at work in human minds and hearts, namely the necessity and yearning to value both the evident and the less evident in the full spectrum of life.

These marks of a sacrament are easily identified. The catechism instructs us that the outward sign in Baptism is water, and the inward signs are union with Christ, adoption into God's church, forgiveness of sins, and new life in God's Holy Spirit. In Holy Communion, the outward signs are bread and wine, and the inward gifts are the Body and Blood of Christ, which offer forgiveness of sins, strengthened union with Christ and with each other, and a foretaste of the heavenly banquet promised in Holy Scriptures.[3]

Faithful participants in these major sacraments often avow that they receive strength for the present, release from the past, and assurance for the future. They view the well-established structures as instituted by Christ himself and as exceptional channels through which transformed life can be validated and nurtured.

To persons who are committed to consider sacraments as exceptional (and occasional) experiences, it might be perplexing to speak of a sacramental universe—a world in which all creation points to the divine Creator and to the graciousness that is to be found in that creation. I shall not enter such debate but simply note that the latter view is expressed in the title of a book, Alexander Schemann's *The World as Sacrament*.[4] I admit that I find the world-as-sacrament point of view very compelling; the opposite view seems inadequate to explain the world as I experience it. Jean-Pierre de Caussade, a Jesuit who lived in France during 1675–1751, eloquently argued that there are true sacramental marks in the commonplace objects and events of everyday human life.

His spiritual counsel to a group of Nuns of the Visitation was recorded and issued after his death, and later translated into English under the title, *Self-Abandonment to Divine Providence*.[5] This book proved to have great influence on contemplative religious and others in France, as well as in English-speaking countries. His central theme is abandonment of oneself to God in trust and love, though a recent English translation bears as its title the subtitle of a section in earlier translations: *The Sacrament of the Present Moment*. [6] Caussade's thought can be viewed as an outline of mystical theology that illuminates the sacrament of the everyday. Though the major theme is that of the abandonment of oneself to God's plenitude of love, I shall focus on his other two themes: the sacramental nature of the everyday and of the present moment.

An observation that Caussade makes early in the book may bring a smile to the reader as it does to me when I realize that he spoke about two hundred fifty years ago.

> God still speaks today as he used to speak to our fathers, when there were neither directors nor methods. Spirituality consisted then in fidelity to the Order of God, but was not reduced to an art, explaining it in so sublime and detailed a manner and containing so many precepts, instructions and maxims as today. Our present necessities demand

this, no doubt. It was not so in those early days
when we were more upright and more simple.[7]

Certainly, many in our day look back to the good old days as
did Caussade.

But Père de Caussade was not naive; for example, he
recaptured Augustine's thoughts on restlessness, descriptive
of our present-day anxieties as well as Caussade's.

Do you expect to find peace by struggling against
the Almighty? Is it not rather this very struggle
that we renew only too often, almost without our
admitting the fact to ourselves, the cause of all our
vain agitations?[8]

And he anticipates questions about how this rest in God
may take place.

You are seeking the secret of belonging to God,
dear souls? There is no other than to make use of
everything which God gives you.[9]

The Special Nature of the Present Moment

Moreover, Père de Caussade several times suggests a
viewpoint that is hard for our ears to hear.

What happens to us at each moment by God's
Order is precisely what for us is the holiest, the
best, the most divine thing that could happen.[10]

John Chapman, a twentieth-century Benedictine abbot, echoed this wisdom in a letter he wrote about prayer
in 1928.

> Don't ask or worry about any kind of prayer or
> recollection or union, but wish for exactly what
> God provides for you *at any given moment.* "Take no
> thought for the morrow." Trust in God. You are
> at each moment in touch with Him through all
> the arrangements of His Providence, and these
> include your own state and your own feelings at
> the moment that you are trying to unite your-
> self with His Will. If you do your best, at that
> moment, the result (however dry, weak, unsatis-
> factory) is just exactly what God wants you to have
> here and now.[11]

Père de Caussade is unwilling to reject any of life's events
because of their simplicity or ordinariness,[12] nor does he see
need of abnormal or extraordinary divine favor.[13] Indeed,
he is able to say (in the title to a subsection of the book),
"The revelation of the present moment is an ever freshly
springing source of sanctity."[14] Caussade's words encourage
each of us.

> The revelation of the present moment is more
> useful because it is addressed personally to us.[15]

> Set aside what is said to others, listen to what is
> said to you for your own use: you will find enough
> to exercise your faith.[16]

Much of what Caussade has to tell us might appear
downright facile, especially when we feel most pressured or
are actively searching for quick answers. We need to keep in
mind that his counsel was addressed to contemplatives.
David Knowles, an English Benedictine of this century,
emphasizes this point in his introduction to Thorwold's
1933 translation.

In his *Letters*, indeed, we see how he speaks to beginners, and those not in religion, but *L'Abandon* is addressed in its entirety to souls of whom he is certain—chosen souls, contemplatives.[17]

Thus it may be presumptuous, if not misleading, for us to attempt a direct acceptance of some of the secondary but important themes, notably sacrament of the everyday or sacrament of the present moment, without being prepared for self-abandonment to God's care, which "may be taught and practiced by repeated acts." Knowles continues.

But 'self-abandonment' in Caussade's vocabulary means something more. It means the real, effective gift to God of all the powers of the soul. It means the attitude, the outlook of a soul so given. It means the state of a soul caught up, so to say, in God's machinery, for which the supernatural life is more real than the natural.[18]

Sacramental Dimensions of the Ordinary

Because there is a common tendency today to lift out of context some of the concepts that we expect will serve our immediate desires, we might be led to conclude that our attentiveness to nature will provide all of the worship we need, or that meditation on our personal experiences will supply all of the requisite prayerfulness for our lives. I urge that we continue regular meditation and corporate worship, thereby supplementing—but not replacing—the human expressions that our spiritual ancestors have passed on to us. These expressions include such insights as the necessity for community as well as for solitude, action as well as reflection, activity as well as rest, a deep concern for ministry beyond self, current events as well as Holy Scriptures—and a host more.

With these cautions in mind, I offer several examples of how the sacramental nature of the everyday can be recalled and valued in our own lives. I seek to exemplify how reflection on the everyday can enrich our lives in community—certainly it should not become a new religion for us. I also seek to assist newcomers in the practice of reflection, initially simply to become more comfortable with the possibility that much of what we experience in everyday life is a channel to giftedness, to the abundance that was mentioned earlier, and to personal experience of the plenteous love that God extends.

I offer three examples to suggest that objects, events, and persons can be channels for God's movement. As examples of the first sort, wedding rings and apple pies can illustrate how objects may give us insight about the sacramental nature of life.

The Book of Common Prayer considers Holy Matrimony a sacramental rite, not necessary for all persons in the way that the sacraments of Baptism and Holy Communion are. Matrimony is described as a sacramental sign of union in heart (the very center of each person's being), body, and mind. Christian marriage is intended, among its other intentions, to point to the union between Christ and the church; presumably to suggest in a visible union (marriage) that the less evident union between Christ and the church is not only possible but potentially enriching. Thus there is an element that cannot be appropriated solely by a wife and husband. How this can be true is a mystery. (But, so is much else about a marriage! I marvel often that in marriage there is the discovery that the more one knows about one's spouse, the greater is the realization of an infinitude yet to be known. Through this realization, the present invites me into the future.)

Moreover, I learn that marriage (or any deep friendship) points to the mystery of otherness, reminding me that no matter how much I know about another person, she or he remains "other"—an original not to be fully understood by any other human being. And I come more and more to understand what is meant by God being "other"—one whom I cannot capture and make conform to how I conceive that God should be. Volumes have been written about marriage, but it remains an experience from which the mystery should not be stripped, even if that were possible. So it is with all that is sacramental. There can be certainty even in the presence of uncertainty and that which can be neither proved nor disproved. One cannot prove the love of another but can experience such love most fully.

What can we say about marriage as sacrament? Recollecting the six marks of a sacrament as given in the catechism, we ask first what are the outward and visible signs? Some would nominate the wedding ring as the evident sign. That is too narrow an understanding for my liking and too dependent upon customs about how rings are worn. My nomination as the visible sign would be the presence of the two people to each other, a presence not limited to physical, visible togetherness but nonetheless symbolized by it. And what of the inward, spiritual gifts and their source, whether from the Lord Jesus or not? I am convinced that my wife was more given to me (and vice versa), than merely the result of romantic arts or irresistibly fine planning on my part (or hers). Was our marriage ordained by Christ? That I cannot prove or disprove, but I do sense that a graceful orderliness has accompanied our prayerful sharing, along with practical planning and childlike playfulness. Is there a sense that the marriage has been a means of receiving giftedness? Yes! In marriage I cannot be only giver but find myself receiver as well. There is much deeply sacramental about marriage, and the wedding ring can be a reminder of that truth.

Now, what of apple pies promised for discussion: can they be channels for giftedness or sacramental signs? I vote yes, visualizing as I do a scene in which someone lovingly prepares the pastry in anticipation that it will be enjoyed by those whom she or he loves. The pie, which is certainly, visible, tasteable, etcetera, can be the means for expressing love in the joint product of God's creation and the effort of human hands. There can be warm appreciation of that love during the time when the pie is being prepared, especially if the baker is present to the way the pastry feels, thereby experiencing the doing and not merely intent on getting the job done. There is a deep question herein for those who are subject to functionalism: How much are we present during our work, and how much of our activity is only to get something over and done with? Objects thus can be seen as true sacraments when we are present to them; our presence allows us to become aware of their true reality, that which is visible and that which is invisible.

The second example, that of event as sacrament, comes from a personal experience that came at a very painful period of my life. Early one November morning, I was walking alone on the grounds of a monastery located in the Mojave Desert of California. I was very much aware of deep loneliness, indeed of bereftness, for my wife Alice had died slightly more than two months earlier. We had often walked together in the quiet immensity of that place, and those memories were among many that filled my mind. The time was approaching 8:00 A.M., still within the period of the Grand Silence, which is regularly observed from the close of the service of Compline on the previous night through the end of breakfast the next morning. I walked from a garden of trees, grass, and flowers that had been established twenty years before on the brown desert terrain. Nothing I saw or heard seemed capable of entering my silence or pain, but as I moved slowly from the garden to the place where breakfast would be served, my eyes turned left and beheld a splendid sight. The object of my attention was a juniper bush, perhaps eight feet wide and four or five feet high. The bush stood in silhouette at the top of a nearby ridge; it was distinguished from the other junipers by its appearance of being vividly afire!

Later thoughts would explain that the needles of the bush were coated with thin layers of ice resulting from nature's response to low temperature and humid air, but such details were, graciously, to be realized only later. The sun's ascent from sea level had begun eighty minutes earlier, but had been hidden behind a more distant ridge. At the moment of my turning, the sun, the bush, and my eyes were in perfect alignment so that the sun was not clearly visible as an orb, but only its reflected brightness could be observed. Such loveliness was not to be easily rejected, and for some time I slowly lowered my head in order to maintain eye, bush, and sun in linear alignment. Then I became aware that my right knee was touching the earth. I was genuflecting in the desert!

After a moment of near-embarrassment about my posture, I realized that I was standing on holy ground, and there came to me in a rush the image of Moses near a bush on Mount Sinai. In time, I realized that the juniper bush was holy, not because I was standing on a holy mountain or because I was on the grounds of a monastery, but because I had permitted myself to appropriate—to be present to—the morning's splendor.

For much of that morning, I thought about the dazzling juniper bush, of Moses before another bush, and about the burden of loss and aloneness that lay upon me. Somehow collecting and embracing these and other jumbled thoughts was the assuring awareness that the same God who had been present to Moses was also attending to myself; that the divine I AM is also I WILL BE, not only in Hebrew history but also in my life. The painful recent past and present moments were connected assuringly to an unknown but inviting future. I did not need to analyze or question whether this graceful encounter exemplified how the present moment can be an ever-flowing source of holiness, as Caussade's written legacy assures us. I was given the conviction of the close connection between the concepts of holiness and wholeness. From that event in which the presence of the Holy One was so strongly felt, I received a sense of well-being, as if I had been led through a painful experience and was being restored—I am brash to say "being put back together."

I urge the reader to imagine how another person in her or his life might be "an outward and visible sign of an inward and spiritual grace given to us, ordained by Christ himself, as a means whereby we receive the same, and a pledge to assure us thereof," again quoting the Anglican Book of Common Prayer.[19]

Our Perspectives Can Change

Perhaps the reader is wondering what all of this has to do with stressful life. "What can I do to fix the problem of excessive pressure in my life?" some might inquire. It is probably misleading to focus on what can be done, unless there is accompanying wonderment of a second question to which the inquirer is willing to be committed: "What sort of person can I be in order to deal more healthfully with a stressful world?" Our commitment to do health-giving actions cannot be separated from change in ourselves.

Earlier we considered the practice of daily, late-morning examination of conscience and consciousness during a coffee break—an inquiry involving very few minutes of time as measured by a clock but often yielding a new perspective and a fresh start. Does this renewed vitality arise simply from the disciplined pause, or is it because I am willing to release? We are not seeking explanation but simply the *is*-ness of that which is appreciated. Hence I might ask whether I experience renewal in what I do and who I am. Do I sense that my formerly limited outlook on life has truly changed? Have my limiting horizons been expanded? The boundary between the visible and the invisible, like the tough or flexible boundaries of the individual self, are far more fluid than we might expect. The discipline of presence in fact changes us so that our interaction with the invisible expands our visible horizons.

In the technical terms to which I referred earlier, we can recapture the vital dimension of life (and feel more back together), and the dimension of the transcendent becomes evident. For a moment, we are lifted beyond the functional dimension and given a sense of living in a universe that is much fuller than we had perceived before. The former repetitive cycle is broken; there is the added gift of restored life. Our willingness to break the steady pattern of busyness has allowed something new to enter. Minisabbath does prove to be a holy rest.

There are indeed clear pointers to more than we were sensing in our activity. We receive a new perspective. The limitations under which we struggled (e.g., "I am just too busy to do anything else," or "One of these days I'll find my way clear to _____.") seem to have receded. We are reminded, even if fleetingly, that the limits and the specific situations of our lives are not the full story. There is a changed perspective, a suggestion that more exists than we now see and that what seems to be a limitation in life is in truth a limited view of our lives. Indeed, extending beyond our new way of perceiving is an expectancy or, I dare to suggest, a near-certainty or foretaste of what can be. We can, in other words, perceive the marks of sacrament in our own lives: countless outward expressions of our lives, the perception of new inward gifts, and a conviction that Christ is very much involved in a transformation that opens us more and more with an increasing certainty about the future.

These changes in vitality and viewpoint, along with a childlike expectancy, suggest that the experience of being present to life is not simply a matter of mastering a situation, but also of being opened to receive. That is perhaps the most surprising of the gifts, a surprise that befits a tiptoeness of expectancy so that one is prepared to receive the fullness of gifts yet to come. The vitality might be part of the preparation for the reception. Certainly, the sense of the giftedness is at the same time humbling and exalting. The writer Thomas Traherne's life (1637–1674) was enriched by his disposition of childlike openness:

> the new and thrilling discovery of the divinity of childhood—that discovery which forms the basis of all the thinking of Traherne. To be able to look upon the world as something wonderfully fresh and beautiful and fascinating, to feel that it all belongs to you and yet to have no desire to call anything in it your own, but to be content to possess it by loving it and understanding it, and thus to create in your own mind a second creation more glorious than the first, because you have given it a voice to praise God and have thus helped him to realize his design in the first creation—this, declares Traherne, is the secret of childhood and we must recapture it if we are to attain true felicity. 'Certainly Adam in Paradise had not more sweet and curious apprehensions of the world, than I when I was a child,' he exclaims.[20]

The commentator concludes that, "This discovery of . . . Traherne was quite as important as any of those made by the Royal Society."[21]

In no way am I suggesting that life is always rosy or that one can turn on and off either divine gifts or our ability to receive them. But after a long, painful period one cannot help but feel humble that such a reversal has occurred. Nor can one deny that the fullness of what follows the pain is cause for happy thanksgiving. Whatever the circumstances there should be a reminder: This is how it can be, even in the midst of busyness and stress.

10
Being Faithful to the Signs

I have asserted that life provides much data about how each of us is continually changing. Countless events and our encounters with other people and objects strongly influence the future shape of our lives. And while we are neither totally independent of these events and encounters nor totally in control, our involvement with them helps to form the nature and the context of later encounters—as well as how we are affected by future interactions. We do not interact with something other than ourselves without undergoing change, be the change ever so slight or gradual.

We must learn to live in a stressful world while not being totally conformed to nor forcibly shaped by the pressures involved in ordinary living. After several decades of life, it should become obvious to each of us that we must find a balance within the pressure, for we can neither take total control nor be totally passive while being ourselves. That balanced interaction constitutes the arena in which our ongoing redisposition takes place.

The decisions about how we respond to life are ultimately ours and must come from within ourselves. We cannot simply respond to "shoulds" imposed by others, nor always be subject to impulses that lead us to seek momentary pleasure. No external source will provide the answers while assuring our very personal sense of well-being; the source must be the original, God-known person each one of us is and is becoming.

This concept of origin and originality might not be easily accepted by readers who are not ready to accept God's presence in their lives, let alone to deal with the mystery of God's action in their creation. I suggest that persons with such cautious viewpoints (which I would not trample!) at least consider that events and human relationships interact in both exterior and interior ways and that the inner person's history extends back in time before her or his own awareness. Admitting such a possibility might allow a new view of mystery, whether or not one views personhood as some preconscious event of which God is the origin. I suggest that the most evident course for investigating our ability to cope in a stressful world begins where we are today, then continues with regular assessments as we experience life. I mean *experience* in its most basic sense of experimenting—attempting, trying, and risking life to the extent that it is open to change, if not also transformation. We can, for example, often be conscious of how our bodies are responding to a situation and to what extent our response is reasonable. We can be aware of whether memory about similar situations cautions us or gives a go-ahead and whether conscience is reluctant to allow us to follow the first response that comes to our awareness.

One difficulty arises in letting life proceed and seeking to be attuned to its course: The evidence is seldom clear until after the incident has passed, and we can only look back on the outcome. While our reflection informs the future, we might not be aware that it is helping in the present (no more than we are conscious at any present moment of slow physical growth taking place). We need to possess an awareness of the present, searching for signals about the directions toward which the present is pointing. If we are serious about our search, we must be sensitive to the signs not only about what has taken place but also about what is still unfolding. That sort of increased awareness is a major subject of this chapter.

Subtle Signs in the Everyday

We cannot effectively deal with the helpful signals in our lives unless we are willing to respond to them. Awareness of the loud, inescapable messages poses little obstacle except for the most resistant among us. Sensitivity to life's more subtle signs, however, requires great openness. This openness not only suggests that change is taking place, but seems to invite vulnerability because we must confront new situations—and that is frightening! But if God is involved in our lives in the way a friend would be involved, and if we truly want to be supported by resources beyond ourselves or even beyond the limits of human resources, we must consider open receptivity.

Our objectives, then, are first to be aware of the signs in our lives and when to investigate how we can be receptive to them. Some of the cowboys in Western novels are adept at "reading sign." They can, for example, ride up to a recently abandoned campsite and by observing hoofprints, bent grass, and scuffed dirt, reliably determine how many people (often the "bad guys"!) were doing what while waiting to depart in another direction to carry out some devilish scheme. While the exploits of these (invariably introspective) readers of "sign" are far-fetched, they illustrate the point that we need to be attentive to the very smallest details in everyday life. Animals survive by being aware of their environments; we also need to be aware of what is taking place—not simply around us but within ourselves as well.

Clearly, it is profitable to consider carefully the signs that emerge in our lives. The Bible indirectly provides us with many examples. We have already noted that the ancient Hebrew tribe probably did a great deal of thinking after recovering from midsummer mussel feasts. Jesus notes that the budding twigs of a fig tree are a sign that summer is coming (Matt. 24:32), and he reminds one audience that they regularly predict weather by the color of the sky (Matt. 16:1–3). The cowboys of my Western stories know, after passing the abandoned campsite, that they will probably ride into an ambush if they continue eastward. (We trust that they will be guided by a reasonable response to the signs and not proceed counter to the indicators out of pure cussedness!)

What are the signs of busyness and stress to which we should be attentive?

We find it difficult to relax and simply do nothing. (Although, it would be difficult for even a small group to agree upon what "doing nothing" means!)

We hurry much of the time and oscillate between high energy and fatigue.

Our children don't ask us to join them in play when they observe that we place our briefcases on the desk in the den, obviously planning to work into the night.

We do not enjoy holidays as much as we used to; on a day off we continue to think about what is happening at the workplace.

Our spouses, friends, and family have ceased raising subjects about which we become defensive.

Both we and our spouses (or significant others) consistently long for more time spent together— no miracles, just more time together.

Reaction or Response to the Signs

Once we become aware of life's subtle messages, a question logically follows. What will be the nature of our decisions and actions in view of the signs? We can either respond in a way that engages us with the indicators and our lives' development (e.g., I might discover that I find supervision more rewarding and should consider it an alternative to my present more remunerative fieldwork). Or, we can react against the indicators, for example working even harder to prove that our fatigue is not connected to our work, as our spouse suggests.

Reaction may be the only effective way to deal with an immediate crisis, but it is an inappropriate way to meet ordinary life situations. We should not proceed in our workaday world (or our hectic home lives) as if each question calls for fight or flight. Reaction, in contrast, is more subject to stimuli and less reflective and thus potentially more likely to mislead in relationships. A more reasoned response, on the other hand, involves us at greater depth and takes place more proportionately to what is occurring. Interestingly, the roots of the words suggest that to react is to turn, bend, or fend off while to respond is to make an offering. Reaction, whether fight or flight, causes us to regard the stimulus or sign as alien and hostile, thus to be overcome or ignored; we refuse in-depth engagement in our eagerness to solve some immediate, short-term issue. In contrast, response allows us to consider the possibility that the sign is helpful and healthful for total well-being, if we are willing to enter into true dialogue with it. Response is relational.

One of the most helpful responses we can make is to listen carefully to the signs in our lives, then to name the demon—the pressure point. Revealing a solitary villain removes our need to be on guard about everything. Even children can deal better with a single, defined monster—say in a movie or story—than a great number of imagined ones.

A special form of listening is required as we consider the wealth of data that life provides and attend to the question of how deeply we are willing to hear. The modes of listening vary according to the nature of the information. For example, the state of our health might become evident as we become aware of specific symptoms. A physician might do some of the listening, noting subtle signs we might miss or being aware earlier than we of what will be discovered. We might become aware of our lessened energy after reflecting on an offspring's outburst, "Oh, you never find time to play catch with me anymore!" Depression could signal a mental health disturbance. (But has the depression surfaced as a result of adrenal exhaustion brought about by incessant busyness or from another source? That question calls for objective assistance.) Certainly, the state of health of marriages and other relationships can speak loudly to us, though we are sometimes more ready to abandon the friendship or marriage (the faithful informant) than to hear the message. We are much too quick to silence the messenger who brings the unpleasant news!

A new sort of awareness (I call it listening) does not just happen without assistance. Deep listening must be learned, and practice is required. We need others who can help us when we are not attentive to ourselves. To call upon others requires a deep level of sharing and openness. Moreover, we need not only the resources of everyday experiences but those of our dreams and aspirations as well. These indirect messages can be quite revealing when we are so overinvolved that our more obvious powers of perception are ineffective. For example, during periods of pressure in my work, my dreams very often take the form of my trying to pack clothing and other items needed for a trip. In each dream, my failure to complete the packing prior to departure time clearly suggests that I cannot find room for anything additional in my life without missing the most important element of the moment.

Mattering as Persons, Not Just as Doers

One of the least attended signs about life is the restlessness that arises out of our hunger for transcendence. I do not
mean the yearning to move from present circumstances to
the idyllic, nor to be at rest, nor even the longing for
atonement with God. Rather, our longing is for the deep,
lived assurance that we matter as persons (and not just for
what we do) and that we are not somehow trapped in the
doings of everyday life. As I suggested earlier, one way of
investigating our restlessness is to inquire whether we are
being true to the original person, the person whom God has
known prior to our own awareness of life.

Many questions have certainly arisen in this discussion! How might we evaluate whether we are truly open
to rediscover and validate the original selves, which once
seemed to be so full of idealism and potential? How might
we return to some of the unsullied innocence—real or imagined—which reminds us that we do not have to fully
conform to the world while living in that world? How might
we come to believe that we are originals and that God
is truly involved in our lives—today as much as ever?
One approach to the question about our originality is to
inquire whether we are acting in accord with God's will
for us. (I shudder to recall the thoughtless misuses of that
term to explain tragedies, hence I simply request that the
reader continue reading.) If we live in harmony with God's
will, we might experience a renewed sense of the specialness
and preciousness of our originality as we become aware of a
continuing sense of well-being, even when daily circumstances are not exactly what we prefer. If, on the other
hand, we do not experience peace and well-being, but restlessness remains, we can rightfully question whether our
way of life is in a true relationship with God. If there is a
close relatedness between God's will for each of us and the
original person each of us was created to be, there should

be a way of identifying with and living more nearly ourselves as originals.

Can it be that we are permitted to approach that state and to experience in life some assurance of drawing near to our original selves? Another way of phrasing the question might be: Does God's Spirit really work within us as individuals and among us? St. Paul would probably answer yes, for in a letter that he wrote to a young church in Galatia, Asia Minor, about A.D. 50 or 60, he lists some indications of how the "fruit of the Spirit" expresses itself in human lives. In Gal. 5:22–23 (RSB), he writes, "The fruit of the Spirit is love, joy, peace, patience, kindness, goodness, faithfulness, gentleness, self-control."

These qualities or dispositions play a very informative role in a long established method for the discernment of spirits:

> The process by which we examine, in the light of faith and . . . of love, the nature of the spiritual states we experience in ourselves and in others. The purpose of such examination is to decide, as far as possible, which of the movements we experience lead to the Lord and to a more perfect service of him and our brothers, and which deflect us from this goal.[1]

The procedure is carefully detailed and applied over a period of many weeks or months with the assistance of an experienced spiritual guide. A basic question asked in the discernment process is whether the inquiring person is moving toward God or away from God. St. Paul's list is called upon to be a "checklist."

For example, I might be assisted in a discernment to determine if my perceived vocation is in harmony with the divine will and expresses my original self. The first question is: Overall, does the experience of work in its present mode bring a sense of love, joy, and peace—not necessarily every day, but a major portion of the time? Am I patient and kind in dealing with others at home and at the market, as well as at my workplace? Am I patient and kind in dealing with myself? If the answer is generally no (i.e., I am not, in the main, patient and gentle in a variety of settings with a sense of joy and peacefulness), there is good reason to question whether my situation is in keeping with the divine concern for me, and I therefore need to reevaluate.

Perhaps I resolve to change the way I interact with my work. After a suitably long period of experience under the new resolve, I should ask myself if there has been a change in the way I view and also live my life. Am I more at peace, more loving and gentle than before my resolve? Do I treat myself and others kindly? If so, I can profitably continue on my revised course. On the other hand, if I experience an increase in pressure and a loss in the dispositions that St. Paul lists, I can judge that the change was not advisable; it seems to be leading me farther away from God's will for me and from the original person I am seeking to rediscover. I live with my feelings, and therefore I need to value my feelings. To do otherwise is to be unaware of or unresponsive to important signs.

But I am not suggesting that these dispositions are the totality of what needs to be considered; they are necessary but not sufficient in making a spiritual discernment. And of course the discernment process might be criticized by persons who want decisions to be made on the basis of what can be quantified and measured. Obviously, that is not always possible (though, admittedly, a spouse might correctly point out that one has been crabby five mornings in a row!). My concern is that every human being is adept at self-delusion; thus we need some sort of objective test if we are to be faithful to the signs offered to us as we live our lives. We need to call upon the wisdom and candor of other persons who are able and willing to tell us how they view our spiritual movement, as evidenced by how we are living our lives. That person might state: I do see you as quite absorbed in your new work but wonder whether you are finding time to be with your friends. Or, the helping person might inquire: It is evident that you are getting ahead professionally, but are you also being drawn into frequent bickering or caught in rivalries that seem pointless because someone else needs to do battle in order to feel that life is exciting? The intent of this objective view is not to clean up the workplace but to assure that our humanizing dispositions are not overlooked in the excitement of the skirmish!

Resisting God's Offer of Help

If we are not personally picking up the signs that life provides and are unwilling to entrust that discernment to another person, it could be that we are repressing that which we find unpleasant within ourselves, or that we simply want to do things our way (come what may!). These responses do not deal with issues but merely push them aside. Such avoidance or willfulness can lead us to resist the breaking in of goodness into life if we fear that accepting good (say the dispositions noted in Gal. 5:22–23) might involve our giving up control. I believe that much of our haunting restlessness arises from that very resistance. We resist accepting the divine invitation to release juggling activities while longing for a sense of well-being that the proffered gifts can produce in love, joy, peace, and the other dispositions that St. Paul lists. Adrian van Kaam has referred to this refusal of the divine invitation as "upward repression." Upward repression[2] is the refusal of a sensed invitation for deeper relationship with God, if that invitation threatens a loss of autonomy. "Upward" suggests resistance to a "breaking in" of good from beyond oneself—somewhat in contrast to the repression of fear, anger, or other emotions "downward" into one's psyche.

The well-known concept of psychological repression has been written and talked about for many years. I believe that it is helpful to compare the two sorts of avoidance, beginning with the more familiar psychological repression. For example, a child may be angry because of treatment received from a parent or other adult, even if the treatment is health-giving parental discipline that the child views as an infringement of freedom. The child might initially strike out physically, only to learn that the adult's superior strength overrides her or his own strength. The ill treatment (or truly benevolent but firm parental guidance) persists, and the child strikes out again and again. In time, the child can only endure, holding anger in check by stuffing it inside. In due course, the child's feelings of frustration and anger become totally removed from the conscious mind. Then, two decades later, some seemingly unconnected incident reaches into her or his subconscious memories, and there is an outburst of anger. Whereas the conscious mind had removed awareness of the former pain, the unconscious had retained the feelings as strongly as they had been twenty years before, when the child could not find an effective way of dealing with the anger expressively.

One way of looking at psychological repression is to conclude that the child in the example relinquished an element of freedom by acting obediently, by complying and yielding to pressure and greater power. This early forfeiture of freedom is demonstrated in adulthood by the uncontrolled eruption of the repressed anger. The relief brought by conformity in childhood now proves to have been temporary. The obedience (actually compliance) was in accord with the parent's desires but not with the child's.

Upward repression, the refusal of the divine invitation to accept goodness, can be viewed as opposite to the repression of anger just described. The first difference is in the refusal of invitation rather than force. More fundamentally, the difference lies in how freedom and obedience are dealt with—and viewed. We can, in our refusal of goodness, express freedom by acting willfully, as we wish, but we thereby act counter to obedience, which is a deep listening to the signs being offered in our lives.

But this view of obedience deserves explanation. It has become common in recent writings on spirituality to examine the linguistic roots of the word *obedience* (*ob* = to or toward + *oedire* = listen; *oboedire* = listen to). When faced with the signs of increased gentleness within myself, for example, I may act other than gently out of a desire to maintain control, lest there be some hidden conditions that accompany the acceptance of God's proffered gifts. But my refusal is at the cost of not really hearing deeply and accepting what I need more desperately than momentary control. Having chosen my own course and rejected the divine offering (of a new disposition or a deeper relationship with God), I am left with an impulse to continue searching for what I deeply desire but refuse when offered.

Refusal of the divine breaking in is portrayed in the story of the great banquet found in the gospel accounts. The parable describes a grand feast to which many are invited and that many refuse to attend. The reasons potential guests give for declining the invitation sound quite contemporary. One man wishes to be with his bride, another to look at newly purchased land, and a third to test five newly acquired yoke of oxen—translate to read automobile or golf clubs (Luke 14:18ff). Both our preferences and the necessities of life are so demanding that we do not sit down with the Lord to consider the matter nor, incidentally, to be nurtured in the process. In our own era, the fictional character Auntie Mame comes right to the point: "Life is a banquet and most poor _____ are starving to death!"[3]

This is indeed an often-repeated pattern: the personal struggle to put our restlessness at rest, the offering that seems too good to be true, our refusal, and the return of our nagging hauntedness. At some point, we must accept the possibility that an offering is intended for us that is of greater value than single-handedly maintaining control. Of far greater worth is the rediscovery of God's unnegotiable presence in our lives and the divine offer to be a fellow searcher for the special original creation each one of us is. Our persistent hauntedness is, I believe, a continuing reminder that God still cares and is still available and that the original persons we were created to be are still only partially expressed. We are, as C. S. Lewis writes, "like an innocent child who wants to go on making mud pies in a slum because he cannot imagine what is meant by the offer of a holiday at the sea. We are far too easily pleased."[4]

I do not wish to speculate about the details of how refusal and restlessness are related. Perhaps the restlessness arises out of an ongoing ambivalence about sharing life with the Transcendent, so that an important possibility remains unresolved. Although I believe that God is very much involved in relationship with each of us (that is the unnegotiable part), I do not conceive of a God who is cynically observing us and waiting to pounce when certain human flaws appear. An acquaintance of mine argues that God does not use coercive or unfair tactics. Indeed, this friend humorously asserts that such a divine attitude has been true for a long time, even when the language was Latin: *Deus non zappet!*

Two Views of Human Will

We need to examine some of the subtleties in the meaning of will, in addition to obedience and freedom—but not entering into theological exchange to conduct our inquiry, for thorough investigations can be found in volumes written over the centuries. Two greatly different usages of the word *will* bear upon our discussion of stress and restlessness and our refusal of the divine invitation to allay these tensions.

When the word *willful* is used in conversation, we tend to think of defiance or obstinance. *Willing,* on the other hand, suggests a favorable inclination. The noun's two major meanings explain both of the above interpretations. One of the meanings—the less apparent and thus not readily evident in what we do—is that the word *will* describes an underlying power of control over one's own actions, and involves such elements as wishing, intending, and choosing. The second meaning of *will* is that of desire or passion, in the sense of appetite for food or other satisfactions.

Adrian van Kaam distinguishes between two kinds of willing: "the will as fundamental self-orientation and the will as concrete embodiment and execution of this self-orientation."[5] He calls the two "primary will" and "executive will." Regarding primary will, another commentator elaborates that

> the first realm is joined to all appropriate human capacities—mental and physical, intellectual and emotional—to form a seamless whole that pushes me in a particular direction . . . a direction whose end cannot be known. While this realm must, to some degree, remain impenetrable to inspection, its predominant experience is one of freedom—the freedom to think, speak, and act forthrightly and responsibly, without blinking the hazards such freedom entails.[6]

In contrast to this primary will, the secondary, executive will

> more readily permits direct . . . exploration . . . [and] is experienced during the event. No longer an abstraction, will's singularity in this realm can be as obtrusive as my own arm, or my own rage, and its thrust is experienced by me as will. . . . [It] presses toward a particular objective—rather than

a direction . . . roughly speaking, utilitarian in nature. Some objectives, when reached, may turn out to have little utility, while the direction of the will of the first realm may have great utility, though utility is neither its motive nor its purpose. The problem of will lies in our recurring temptation to apply the will of the second realm to those portions of life that not only comply, but that will become distorted under such coercion. . . . I can will knowledge, but not wisdom . . . lust, but not love . . . self-assertion, but not courage . . . religiosity, but not faith.[7]

Van Kaam continues: "Western culture has promoted secondary executive willing often at the cost of primary self-orientation . . . high premium on practical performance and achievement."[8] One of the direst possibilities is that in our busyness we can lose our selves!

These views suggest underlying tensions involved in being active humans and yet faithful to the original creations that we are. The twentieth-century philosopher Paul Ricouer, in a discussion of relationships between choice and motivation, recalls Spinoza's seventeenth-century concept of "inner necessity" as being deeper than any choice and any kind of autonomy.[9] He argues that there is passivity or receptivity at the heart of will "which renders itself sensitive to anything which can incline it without necessitating it."[10]

In commenting about this perspective, Alden Fisher inquires

Is the highest degree of human liberty to be conceived as the independence of human choice, a man's power of deciding for himself, or is it, on the other hand, the discovery and comprehension of an interior necessity, one which is deeper and more profound than any choice? . . . Must not the necessity in question concern the relation of man, of the concrete human existent, to some existent (ultimately personal) beyond himself? . . . [An] internal relation between himself and a transcendence . . . [and] will it not be the case that man may adhere to this relationship freely and voluntarily?[11]

Fisher terms the requisite human response as *receptive volition,* willingness to receive.

These philosophical insights bring into the same arena the triad of obedience, freedom, and will—certainly not a new thought for the reader familiar with theological ideas. A bit more tantalizing, perhaps, is the concept of inner necessity as it relates to the restlessness that seems to accompany the personal search (or lack of search) for the original person each one of us is. So, to summarize the effect of pressured life on our appreciation of both aspects of will: Our common tendency is to express ourselves through executive (action-taking) will. This involves a high expression of control, which we struggle to maintain. An overdevelopment of the dispositions that support this control can cover the signs in our lives that might help us to be obedient to the primary will (our originality or inner necessity). Thus, being aware of life's signs and being obedient to them is not just a matter of practice but also a matter of developing our capacity for primary will—our capacity to receive in relationship. An essential relationship is with the Transcendent; any realistic intention to deal with stressful life must be aware of that truth.

11
Beginning to Say No to Pressure

Are there responses that can creatively bring together the promised presence and cooperation of the Transcendent with the very personal issues of life, some of which have already announced themselves in pressured, stressful ways? Indeed, the operative word needs to be *response*, meaning our contribution to our ongoing formation in ways that are faithful to the evident signs in our lives and receptive to the support of the Transcendent. The matter is clouded because of the strong tendency in our day to *initiate* what we privately classify as spiritual matters. The word *response* suggests (correctly) that we cannot control all of the details of our lives. For example, nature sets the broad context for survival, society imposes conditions that both assist and restrain our preferences, and our own physical health is not totally under the control of our minds.

If we are resolved to remain in charge of how our lives will unfold, we will probably resist suggestions to change our eating or work habits, to join Bible study groups, or to venture away on a silent retreat. Still more threatening would be the suggestion to begin observing a spiritual dis-cipline or to adopt a rule of life. If we reject such spiritual counsel, we will likely also resist sharing any but the sketchiest details about our spiritual pilgrimages and will seek to go it alone. We might be more inclined to "do our part" in our own way and then to call on God to do "God's part" in our partially formulated plan. Just what God is to do might not be thought out well, but often we expect God to either enter our plan as already formulated or, at most, make some appropriate minor modifications. But we are not often wildly enthusiastic for a major engagement with God except under quite extreme circumstances.

This modern preference for self-sufficiency is not a new inclination, for our forebears were challenged on this very point in substantial parts of the scriptural accounts. We are reminded throughout the Bible that God has acted, and humankind is invited to respond to the loving and often mysterious actions of God. Response is what we likewise are to be concerned about; for God has not only acted in history in wide-ranging impersonal ways but very much in our individual lives as well. This reality should remind us that there are no general-purpose solutions that work for everyone. It should remind us that each person is, in St. Paul's words, to "work out your own salvation with fear and trembling; *for* God is at work in you, both to will and to work for his good pleasure" (Phil. 2:12f., RSB; italics mine).

Maybe it has come to the reader's mind that an appropriate response is to adopt certain helpful spiritual disciplines as an opening for the process of cooperation with God. "If I can really shape up in the areas of prayer and Bible reading," some may think, "that should be enough for now." It might very well be true that these or other disciplines will prove to be quite helpful, but disciplines are not a means to control outcomes. While they are very helpful in freeing us from a variety of obstacles, spiritual disciplines should not be considered as direct means to ends. Francis Baur, a Franciscan priest and teacher, opposes the idea that disciplines make one spiritual:

The assumption works in exactly the wrong direction. It is not our practices and our disciplines which have the effect of making us spiritual; on the contrary, it is our spirituality which gives meaning and value to our practices and disciplines.[1]

Cautions about our initiating the search for a changed life should not deter us. We can, so to speak, prepare the way, even if we cannot draw a detailed map. Several dramatic calls to such preparation are found within the scriptural record. For example, in the New Testament, John the Baptist views himself as the way-preparing forerunner of Jesus (Mark 1:2–3). We are familiar with the words that John repeats from his learned tradition: "Prepare ye the way of the Lord," or, in another translation, "Make ready the way of the Lord." John is applying to himself the call issued to all persons to facilitate the return of an exiled people to their homeland— in our day also we are issued a call to return to lives in which we feel home at last.

> A voice cries out: In the desert prepare the way of the Lord. Make straight in the wasteland a highway for our God! Every valley shall be filled in, every mountain and hill shall be made low; the rugged land shall be made a plain, the rough country a broad valley. Then the glory of the Lord shall be revealed (Isa. 40:3–5a, NAB).

This highway metaphor is pertinent to thoughts about inviting the working of God into our lives in an ongoing sense, not welcoming God into our lives only in an initial step of a conversion. God's grace continuously converts our lives, although the changes might seem gradual. The preceding biblical image of the desert highway suggests preparations for a political ruler's visit to remote areas of the realm. Boulders and other hazards are to be removed from the roadway, sharp curves are to be lengthened, dips and peaks to be flattened. However, despite the overstatement in Isaiah's description, the land is not to be devastated to the point of flatness; mountains are not to be totally leveled, nor valleys to become clogged so that waterways disappear. The natural life and scenic beauty are not to be eliminated to facilitate rapid and comfortable movement.

So it is in our preparations: We are to enable God's deepened presence but not at the extremity of removing all of the special dispositions that have already been given to us. Disciplines may thus be viewed not only as abetting the process of God's continued presence and nurture but also as promoting ongoing discovery of our originality—a most important starting point for each of us daily. As the words *origin* or *originate* suggest, something has already been set in motion for each of us. We fail to value that reality at our own loss.

For several reasons, ascetic practices do not work for most human beings. First, there is always the temptation to use such routines as a means of avoiding relationship. Moreover, if we initiate disciplines with the expectation of specific outcomes, they become a controlling ploy and a potential source of disappointment if our chosen projects do not succeed. Such failure can be seized upon to justify abandoning a continued longing for relationship. Finally, we need to be aware that harsh and arbitrary practices might intrude adversely into the rights of others in our lives.

Planning Facilitates Receptivity

Perhaps it is becoming evident that our response to the convergence of God's involvement and human response to pressure will take the form of preparation and receptivity. We are not to present ourselves as some inert offering nor to insist on proceeding independently: The issue is not one of choosing between activity and passivity. Jean-Pierre de Caussade's key word *l'abandon* is translated into English as *self-abandonment*. I am more inclined to use the term *disposition*: We dispose ourselves in the sense of being truly available through putting forth or offering ourselves.[2]

What might be some characteristics of the offering that we can make in disposing ourselves to this divine invitation? I suggest neither passivity nor assertiveness but a dual expression that takes the form of gentle repetition of beneficial acts in harmony with regular reflection that always includes release of the insights to God. Throughout, our intent is not calculative. Our relationship with God must not be treated in a contractual manner that implies, I'll do this, if you will do that, God. (For that matter, we deprive any relationship of mutual respect by expecting outcomes that are not consonant with the being of the other. How offensive, for example, are parental signals that indirectly but quite clearly say, I'll love you *if* you: make me proud at junior soccer games, bring home good grades, don't experiment with drugs, and don't get involved in sex.)

Nor is our cooperation with God an area for the practice of management by objectives (MBO). This organizational development skill has brought efficiency and guidance to corporations and has restored a sense of direction to religious congregations, but the primacy it gives to detailed planning and evaluation has, at the same time, edged God into a corner. In general, MBO deals effectively with problems by moving from generalities to specifics, proceeding from one step to another in the planning only after the preceding area has been thoroughly agreed upon. These steps, in a progression of increasing detail, might be: issues, concerns, goals, objectives, program details, and evaluation. For example:

> The fundamental issue is to provide a product while making a profit.
>
> Our concern is that profits are steadily declining in the production and sale of metallic widgets.

Our goal is to develop a line of plastic widgets similar to the sort of product with which other companies are now claiming a major part of the market.

Our immediate objective is to produce and run market acceptability tests on disposable plastic widgets, which might supplement our present line of heavy-duty steel widgets.

The program will take the following form: design of the product shape will be completed by date A; pilot production by date B; etcetera by dates C, D, and E; market acceptability tests by date F.

Evaluation includes a time line describing which evaluative steps are to be attained by which dates in order to answer the question: Shall we begin full production, advertising, etcetera of plastic widgets?

Personal use of the MBO model finds several expressions among individuals who have found planning life to be far more orderly than just living life in an unexamined way. One popular form of ordering life is economic planning for retirement, a laudable practice. (But this form of planning often needs to be supplemented by attentiveness to aspects beyond the economic ones. For example, as the financial planning proceeds, a spouse might confess to a friend, "I really won't be too unhappy if Alphonse stays on the job. I'm thinking that we also should have planned how best to be with each other all day every day.") Time management, another means of planning life, is also a topic for seminars. (Alas, the guidelines are often forgotten within six months after the seminar because of the time pressures of "putting out fires" in the present job situation.) Career development is also a form of life planning not always initiated by the person but by the corporation that sees promise in the individual and requires certain assignments, training courses, apprenticeships, and social involvements to prepare the worker for middle management befitting the company's objectives.

I am not negative about these several helpful methods of life planning. My reservation is simply that we tend to undertake projects (spiritual disciplines, retirement planning, time management, or career development) in ways that place two elements in conflict: the method that must be used and the outcome that is demanded. This dual requirement is not fulfilled in a great number of human endeavors, and we make serious misjudgments by believing so and thereupon investing our lives in such expectations. I offer the example of an inventor who carefully draws the design of an item and then carries finished blueprints to a machine shop. There he tells the foreman, "Here are my drawings. I ask you to abide by the details closely and I want the finished product to function in a way that I have described for you on this second paper." Of course, a wise shop foreman will say, "We can proceed in either of two ways. First, I am willing to abide by the details of the drawing, but cannot promise the performance you want. On the other hand, if you give me freedom to modify some of the details, I might be able to obtain the performance you wish."

Adapting this analogy to our own lives, we can see the importance of drawing up a guide for our lives. We can recall and respect the long process that led up to the insight of seeing a need for the plan, but the finished outcome of our lives cannot be described so precisely that laborious adherence to instructions will assure the best possible finished product. In the machine shop example, the best course will probably prove to be close communication between designer and shop foreman, which involves the technician

or mechanic fabricating the item. That same frequent communication can be expressed in our ongoing lives through
regular transcendent reflection, prayer, and other health-
giving disciplines that we discover in the course of striving
to live the gently examined life.

Père de Caussade's words of consent to God are essentially, "Do it *your* way, Lord," but that should not suggest
a passivity that expects God to do all. Self-abandonment as
he described it is not an ascetic renunciation of self nor
an assertion of self-will or self-love but acceptance of God's
will and submission to it. To our highly individualistic
society, *submission* is a word that may evoke discomfort.
However, it may mean a lack of presumption or a humble
and patient testing of a given circumstance. David Knowles
illustrates this in his introduction to Thorwold's translation
of *L'Abandon.*

> Two common uses of the word in English may help
> us to an appreciation. We speak of a swimmer
> abandoning himself to the waves or the current.
> He may or may not wish to swim against, across or
> with them; in any case he finds that his independent
> efforts are useless or needless, and he abandons
> himself to the waters. We speak of one abandoning
> himself to grief. From this motive or that, by dis-
> traction or compulsion, with hope of success or
> without it, he has kept grief from mastering him.
> He now opens his heart to it and becomes all grief.
> It masters him and yet it is what his heart desires. If
> we substitute the divine action for the waters of the
> sea or of sorrow in these two phrases, we shall have
> a faint inaccurate description of Caussade's 'self-
> abandonment'—inaccurate because in the case of
> cooperation with grace the human liberty and, at
> least normally, the human effort is still, and must
> be, present.[3]

Caussade reminds us: "This work (of God's spirit) is not accomplished by way of our own cleverness or intelligence, or subtlety of mind, but by way of our passive self-abandonment to its reception."[4] The examples of the swimmer and bereaved person point to several of the dynamics in expressing one's vocation. As grief masters us during a period of bereavement (even as we desire to be fully in the experience), so we are deeply fulfilled in the immersion of vocation. But vocation means that to which we are called and not necessarily that which we are doing! Thus arises the need for ongoing discovery of our originality and consequently our cooperation with God in how life continues to reveal that special person in us.

A distinction between originality and individuality brings this into focus. We speak of an individualist as one who stands on her or his own two feet, who knows what she or he wants and is willing to be assertive in reaching for what she or he seeks. An individual stands out in the crowd and might even promote that self-presence by always moving to the center of attention. Not all of us are individualists, though an extensive study reports that individualism is quite evident among Americans, whereas the commitment to community or a shared cause, which formerly accompanied such persons, is less and less expressed.[5] But, we are all originals—already originals in the sense of being created that way.

As I use the term originality, we all begin as different from others, and our central dynamic remains that of living (or not) in consonance with that originality that is seen as precious enough that one does not set out to create a quite different person. I have suggested that receptivity greatly facilitates the nurture and ongoing formation of the persons we began to be and continue to become and that a restlessness continues if we are not faithful to the original.

The individuality that we all express from time to time seems to arise out of our executive will, in much the way that we set out to establish our own identity. An example of individual identity is actually the composite of several persons I have known. A young woman, trained as an accountant, began work at age twenty-two as a book-keeper and seemed unable to break into a more advanced area of accounting. After four or five years, she and her husband decided to become parents, with the intention that the woman would return to professional work in a year or so. But they then brought forth a second child, and the young mother continued her life at home. After being away from the workplace for almost five years, she took two brush-up courses and was then hired as an accountant. She did well, advancing twice in two or three years. This woman recently commented that she now feels valued for who she is—for the skills she offers, for having reached professional ranks, among other reasons. She has found an identity that was elusive a few years earlier, she says. This enterprising woman freely reminds persons who praise her for her present professional status that she frequently has to assert her position among her colleagues. To a few people she confides that she does not want to slip from her present position but regrets the need to constantly work unpaid extra hours and to assert herself in order to protect the position that she connects with her identity.

Apropos of this example, Tilden Edwards comments about a dominant view today that each of us perceives the need to cultivate a separate ego "to produce, enhance, maintain, or protect this buildup of self. This task, imposed on us both by our culture and ourselves, has an edge of anxiety and striving violence to it. We believe that it is up to us to get and to keep who we are."[6]

Clearly, we are cocreators who both may and must take part in our own unfolding if we are to experience fulfillment as persons. God will not force our discovery. At the very least, we must truly intend to be engaged in our spiritual growth with the assistance of God's Holy Spirit. Curiously, the tensions of life sometimes are the very experiences that seem to lead us to the point of decision or intention. What an interesting play on words in English: we are *in tension*, and out of that tension we make the commitment of *intention*. (In other words, we respond to signals that living itself provides.) And, to make the wordplay even more relevant, it is probably true that we are *tending* to move in a specific life direction because God is already attracting us in that direction! My suspicion is that we often stiffen our resistance at the point just prior to breakthrough and turn back because we sense at some subconscious level that we are about to abandon ourselves to God's invitation. Recall that some alcoholics will find the twelve-step programs (e.g., Alcoholics Anonymous) very attractive but will balk just at the point of admitting their compulsive behavior. In counseling situations, the resistance often becomes intense when discovery of the truth is only one step ahead.

I need not belabor the point that some persons truly want to put to rest their stressful lives, and others do not. But each of us can profit by inquiring about our motivations with such questions as: Am I seeking only to solve a problem, or am I also willing to appropriate the mystery called life?

12
Ongoing Checkpoints

In previous chapters I have not offered formulas for solving problems of stress or for explaining mysteries, but rather I have encouraged the reader to enter the mystery of life in an intentional but gentle way. Instead of providing a how-to manual, I have sought to lift up foundational elements that I believe will illuminate several persistent, basic concepts (and misconceptions) that may lie beneath an undervaluing of our lives and health. Several of the concepts have been self-evident. Perhaps some readers have brushed aside other views as being unacceptably speculative. I now risk repeating some of the self-evident concepts by listing seven considerations for persons who wish to personalize them by testing them in their own experience.

Stopping busyness—an intentional alternative to continued activism

Listening beyond the internal and external noise in our lives

Being receptive in a way that goes beyond dependency and the attitude of entitlement

Sharing in relationships what has been received spiritually as well as in other ways

Appraising, meaning an appreciation that issues from one's availability to look candidly at life

Balancing—which is quite different from juggling an overload

Beginning anew

Stopping

To stop activity signifies not merely a cessation from what one is doing but also a quieting of internal busyness as well. Such a pause should be intentional in order to be a true sabbath (though perhaps a minisabbath in duration), but in any case it should be an opportunity to recognize not only the act of creating but the mystery of creation as well. The experience of intentional stopping allows one to put activity on hold and to let a new fullness of time be experienced during the clock time that more often claims our attention. The ease or difficulty in beginning and nurturing this intentional effort will likely prove to be very informative. Like a large ship under way, we cannot always change course or bring our fully laden routines to a halt simply by deciding to do so!

What if one is already on a right course? All the better! In cessation of routine, we come to value that course and remain receptive for more of what has been supportive and life-giving. There is deep truth in the assuring words of Jesus: "For to him [her] who has will more be given" (Matt. 13:12 RSB). (Though for years thinking this statement as tolerating inequities, I have come to realize that we can freely and responsibly use what is given to us, in the assurance that we shall not deplete our gifts. I am willing to go further, in asserting that an excellent way to thank God for life is to enjoy and share the life that is given.)

By trial and error, I have discovered that the best time for me to be quiet and reflective is very early in the morning, before busyness has taken charge of the day. In a sense I stop before I start. But other times are too filled with necessities involving other people, and to wait for quiet reflection until the end of the day is like giving the dregs to God and self. Thus, I set aside at least a half hour for quiet prayer and reading the Bible, with further time for reconnecting with the world of nature. If I fail to do this, I am aware later in the day that something important is missing. A feeling of emptiness comes as surely as hunger will come if I should fail to have breakfast. For the past two decades, I have realized that I have been setting aside prime time for the quiet periods, for I am very much a morning person who feels energetic early in the day. I have heard many times that persons who willingly tithe money (e.g., ten percent of income for charitable purposes) seldom forsake that practice. So it has seemed for me with time as well as with money. Moreover, when the day starts gently, so it often continues. But even when the practice is regular, a mystery remains: When I begin the day by setting aside time for inactivity, additional time somehow seems to be given to me!

Listening

Listening has been discussed in detail earlier, hence the reader is already aware that hearing includes attentiveness to the subtle signs and yearnings of life as well as the evident aural sense. In the preceding paragraphs, the cessation of busyness and stressful living habits was likened to stopping the forward movement of a large ship. To continue in the nautical metaphor, we sometimes can simply let the momentum decrease. At other times, the propelling forces must be put in reverse. And if we are to rest in a safe mooring place, we need to be attentive to the external forces—the currents and winds. Obviously the exact entrance and positioning in a busy channel (our complex world) can profitably utilize the expert guidance of a person who knows the strange new area being approached—and perhaps a few appropriate nudges (which, of course, the pilot and tugs provide in my example). We are fortunate if we have such helpful persons in our lives. If not, we can at least understand that a guide who has already experienced much of what we now encounter is much more helpful than a formula or a map for living.

Stopping and listening should remind us that we cannot be in constant movement or activity. Persons who can't stop right now should be very clear about exactly when and how they plan to do so. If an appointment book is used, it would be helpful if several occasions for stopping are marked well ahead, preferably written in large letters in ink.

Receiving

We are most ready to receive when we are receptive—an obvious truth, unless we view life as a relay race in which the batons are passed while we are running our fastest. (The latter sort of reception indeed sometimes occurs unplanned and is called heart attack, stroke, or a variety of other names.) To be receptive means to be open so that newness can be admitted. For some of us, however, receptivity suggests admission of another sort, namely that we are not self-sufficient. The very thought of dependency on others is unacceptable to some people, who seem not to understand that being able to depend on other persons can also be very freeing. I look upon such an avoidance of dependence as regrettable, having learned that much of my "independence" arises from a willingness to trust God, my wife, and a host of others—known and unknown. Such trusting dependence (truly it is interdependence) is very liberating, even as it reminds me that I am not some sort of free-floating entity in the universe.

The receptivity I am discussing is by no means passive; rather there is a resonance between giver and receiver. The one who receives love becomes lovable and is more likely to be capable of loving. Imagine the parents of a small child who has entered one of those phases that seem to test parental patience and gentleness to the utmost. The child acts so obstreperously that she or he rapidly runs through the list of what can be done by parents in such cases. The adults are at the point of becoming physically violent but remain patient and lovingly firm. Then, after days or weeks or months, the child seems quickly to become gentle and affectionate. Such a blessing, such a mystery! But is not the child exhibiting the qualities that have been experienced, and indeed returning a portion of what has been given—and received?

Consider another example of a person who has been endowed with the gift of a body that seems more to flow than to walk. The lightness of step becomes evident at a very early age and is nurtured by discerning parents who provide the funds, the transportation, and the inevitable calendar rearrangements necessary to make dancing lessons possible. Assume that the long training bears much good fruit. If the child comes to value this talent as a gift, a graciousness that adds to the physical gracefulness will likely follow. If, on the other hand, the gift is not thus viewed and accepted, some antisocial traits born of precociousness may become evident. This example illustrates how the trusted, lived-out experience of receptivity as openness to ongoing giftedness is important to our spiritual nurture.

Obviously, there are many attitudes exhibited in how people accept gifts of any sort—gifts from nature, the manufactured goods of the world, or the ministrations and services of others. Some treat the environment as if it is a sensitive friend, while others seem uncaring in their abuse of a delicate ecological balance. Some expect to get what they pay for in services, while others recognize that the servants (physicians or porters or parents) are also persons and not merely providers. Americans are sometimes stereotyped by citizens of other cultures as people who voraciously consume in order to produce and consume and thus be called upon to produce still more. Among the young, there has emerged a viewpoint sometimes referred to as the "entitlement ethic," in which each individual is entitled to comfort and luxury irrespective of requirements for labor, sharing limited resources, or a subsequent expression of gratitude or stewardship. Such grasping is, of course, antithetical to the receptivity of spiritual gifts.

The English language can assist our understanding of how gifts are accepted in attunement with their true source. God's grace (expressed in the giftedness of daily life—the bestowal of life itself and the experiences of persons, things, and events, for example) is received gracefully, without question or hesitancy. Grace received gracefully leads to a grateful heart (abundantly filled, as well) that expresses the person's gratitude. Thus does a person become gracious, in a transformation no less real than that of the willful child who moved from combativeness to docility by her or his own choice. Such transformation points to the cocreation of loveliness by God and responsive persons. How well it demonstrates that life is not to be taken for granted but received as a grace!

Sharing

Deep sharing of our lives with God can begin with the emergence of gratitude and graciousness in response to

God's graceful offering of gifts to all of us. So graceful, in the sense of hiddenness and gentleness, is God's giving that we need to do some of our sharing in an intentional manner that at least recognizes the possibility that God might be involved in our lives. Prayer is one mode of sharing our lives with God about which thousands of books have been written in English alone during this century. But praying can be done, no matter how clumsily, more rewardingly than it can be thought about in reading or writing.

I find it helpful to consider prayer in terms that describe some of the dynamics of any close friendship. Five factors are apparent in friendship: appreciation of the relationship, deep confidence, mutual nurturing, awareness that the friendship is a special relationship for each of the two persons, and never-completed experiences, which will draw the friends back to each other's company at a future time. The latter is certainly an element that both nurtures and gives ongoingness (i.e., life) to friendship, for it bespeaks an abundance in the relationship.

These five marks of friendship could have been written as the five expressions of prayer that have been taught for centuries: adoration, confession, petition, intercession, and thanksgiving. One way of expressing adoration is to release in joy whatever goodness comes to heart and mind. Such appreciative praise is itself a confession of belief that God is in our lives. The deep confessional sharing of fears and faults can come later if there is reason for present hesitation. Petition, the request for assistance and guidance, indicates an openness and longing for life to be enriched. This help comes naturally in friendship, of which prayer is a special expression. Intercession allows others to share our friendship as we pray in heartfelt concern for them. Thanksgiving expresses an abundance and, as in any friendship, makes known the desire for ongoingness: I can't possibly fit it all in this one meeting, Lord, and I look forward to our next meeting. Clearly, prayer has many of the same dynamics as human friendship. Prayer helps to deepen our friendship with God, for prayer is not a one-way expression.

Most of the examples in this book have focused on the ongoing formation of individuals. I have discussed how life is shared with God by always releasing, by handing back to God the insights and unresolved issues of our reflections on life and its particulars. I strongly assert that life is neither so simple nor so private that our reflections and transformed lives can be shared by mere thought waves that issue from prayerful meditation. The sharing that we must experience is necessarily a sharing with other human beings in all expressions of our lives. Indeed, this one point deserves as much discussion as has already been presented in this book!

Appraising

Appraisal is the word I have chosen to convey not only the evaluation of ongoing life but a valuing of life as well; this is similar to what Mary of Nazareth does in the second chapter of Luke's gospel account. After the shepherds have departed from beholding the newborn Jesus, Mary ponders the decription of the angelic message they have heard in the fields and continues to treasure the experience. Such appraisal can occasionally supplement a much more frequent reflection on everyday experience. A particularly helpful practice for me is to review my journal at year's end while on retreat. Some persons (in decreasing numbers, I suspect) make formal confessions on a regular basis. Still another helpful procedure is to meditate about personal responses to a list of questions. I encourage readers to meditate now on the following list.

How helpful am I in maintaining my physical health?

Am I consciously trying to continue my intellectual growth?

What am I doing to nurture close personal relationships?

How well do I manage time? Are my days consistently crammed?

Do I regularly break patterns of steady activity? Daily? Less frequently?

What in life is most fulfilling for me?

Are my major commitments helping to move me in the direction of fulfillment?

Do I sense God's involvement in my major commitments?

Have I asked God (in prayer or otherwise) to be involved in my major commitments?

What are my major disciplines?

What additional discipline might I find helpful?

In what ways am I most likely to sabotage regular health-giving disciplines?

What activity might it be helpful to eliminate? (A guideline to be considered is this: If I feel urged to add some discipline, what am I prepared to relinquish in order that the new may truly be nourished, and not merely become an addition to an already full life?)

How seriously do I relate to St. Paul's words: "If the Spirit is the *source* of our life, let the Spirit direct the *course* of our life?" (Gal. 5:25, NEB; *emphasis mine*). Note that the same letters make up the words "source" and "course," a lovely coincidence that might help us to remember that God not only originates but continues to accompany and nurture us.

An example from my own life will illustrate some bene-fits that can come from regular appraisal. For a number of years, my wife, Norvene, and I have observed what we call a monthly day of recollection. Typically, we visit the same monastery for a period of about twenty-seven hours, arriv-ing in time for worship at Vespers (6 P.M. evening prayer) with the monks and departing after supper the following day. We find it refreshing to have a change of setting away from home and telephone, to awaken in a desert ambience, and especially to reconnect with old friends, human and inanimate—including the Transcendent One!

We are able to "recollect" ourselves in several senses of the word: remembrance, integration of daily experiences during the preceding month, reflection on insights that invariably come (most easily, it seems, during motionless meditation for Norvene and in the course of unhurried walking for myself). Before we began sharing these days, I had visited the same monastery many times. I should like to say that I had done so regularly, but the truth is that I usually went there on a few days' notice every three or four months. After our marriage, we agreed to visit once per month. On our departure at the end of our first visit together, we set a date for the next time, and we have continued that practice. After the first six monthly visits, I realized that my overall valuing of the day of recollection had increased considerably. Years ago when I began regular monthly visits, I had usually gone with a mixture of relief and of escape from a busy life. On a deeper level, I realized that I was rewarding myself for my work. Truth to tell, I had been rewarding myself for overwork—not a commendable practice of reinforcing a pressured work routine! With the regular schedule planned in advance, I have come to realize that I experience a buildup of excitement and expectancy, which I feel and savor for several days prior to the visit, whether or not I consult the calendar. And I have been made aware once more that freely accepted disciplines can be liberating.

Balancing

A variety of today's literature strongly advocates a holistic view of of the earth, suggesting that nature is best understood as an interaction rather than a summing of the atmosphere, oceans, land, plant life, animal life, human beings, and the other elements that make up the physical world. Likewise, in the holistic view, human life cannot be compartmentalized into spiritual life, professional life, family life, sex life, church life, community life, etcetera. Activity in each of these expressions directly affects the other expressions. In the larger natural world, there is a strong interaction between, for example, atmosphere and the ability of plants to thrive or even survive, or between human-released pollutants and a destruction of the protective ozone screen, which heretofore has kept ultraviolet radiation within endurable limits. So it is with our lives; our lives cannot be compartmentalized without having adverse effects on the person.

The holistic view of human life suggests the importance of living in a way that the several essential elements are not in ongoing conflict. Our physical, mental, and spiritual needs are interactive and, it is hoped, mutually supportive. We might most readily reach agreement on the need for some sort of balance between our essential elements by considering several caricatures. For example, the so-called bookworm is faulted for being out of touch with the world because so great an emphasis is given to mental preoccupation. As regards the physical aspects of life, magazine photography shows us the finished product of bodybuilding, complete with tanned skin that has been oiled to a shining finish just before facing the camera. Spiritual athletes also exist, I am reminded by a modern folk song: "you're so heavenly minded, you're no earthly good."[1] Whether or not these caricatures are fairly drawn, they remind us that we are all undivided personalities who must necessarily be attentive to a principle of balance in attending to the three elements of each person bequeathed to us by ancient philosophical thought: body, mind, and spirit.

The importance of balance in life is stressed in the Rule of St. Benedict, which after almost fifteen hundred years remains a remarkably current guide for the well-ordered life. The three vows made by Benedictine monastics (women as well as men) are stability, obedience, and openness to conversion of life.[2] (Unwittingly, I approximated the essence of these vows in the first three listings as stopping, listening, and receiving.) The Rule specifies that four hours be spent daily in liturgical prayer, four hours in study and meditation, and six hours in manual work. If the portions of the day set aside for prayer and study seem excessive, we may recall that the time segments were established long before schools were generally in existence. The evident intent is clear: to nurture spirit, mind, and body in a balanced way.

Many adults today are sensitive to the need for a well-rounded diet. The Rule of St. Benedict reminds us that the full person requires balanced nurture in additional respects, and adherence to the Rule demonstrates that the elements of daily life are brought into a proportion that is experienced as a harmony. Esther de Waal, British historian of Benedictine and Celtic spirituality, writes that balance helps one "to become more fully, totally human, by recognizing that all the elements of our make up are God-given and equally worthy of respect."[3]

Among Christians living outside of monastic settings, there is also a long tradition of "rules of life" being observed by individuals to provide a balanced and disciplined way of life. Briefly described, such rules are plans for organizing energy and time so that maximum spiritual nurture can be realized. The most obvious example is that of a written rule that sets forth a daily schedule, which the person discovers will provide safeguards against over-busyness and the consequent loss of attentiveness to harmony in life. If the rule is to be truly helpful, it must be specific and detailed enough to support the person's resolution yet flexible enough to accommodate unforeseen change in circumstances.

For adults, as for young children, human formation prospers within a supportive structure elastic enough that it does not become burdensome or something only to be tolerated. A helpful rule of life arises out of what is discovered to be nurturing. Initially, the details may be suggested by what others have found to be helpful, but in the end a rule of life must be consonant with the individual's deepest needs. In that sense, a rule is not so much a listing of commandments as a helpful inventory to refer to regularly and conscientiously—a measuring device rather than a rigid listing of stringent requirements.

Following is a format that I have found to be helpful in taking periodic inventory of disciplines in my life. I have inserted several examples to emphasize the importance of being specific in each category. The list is surely daunting! A beginner will be well advised to adopt just a few of the disciplines at the outset and to all others as their helpfulness is discovered. I use three guidelines to prepare my inventory: entries should be as specific as possible; choices should reflect structure and flexibility; and provision should be made for accountability to self.

MY PERSONAL RULE OF LIFE
To be used for regular inventory of my life disciplines

Date_____

Care of Self

- Personal health (diet, exercise, rest, therapy)
  (For example, jogging for fifteen to twenty-five minutes
  five days per week)

- Mix of vocation and avocation

- Leisure, solitude, silence in the context of activity

- Prayer, both contemplative and intercessory

- Patterns of meditation, reflection, study
  (For example, monthly day of recollection)

- Friendship and intimacy
  (For example, taking the initiative for involvement in
  at least one social function each month)

- Self-examination and confession

- Other

Life in a Worshiping Community

- Participation in liturgical life
  (For example, weekly attendance)

- Leadership in my primary worshiping community and volunteer work in a nonleadership role

- Participation in group retreats, study, service, etcetera

- Receiving objective guidance by another person
  (For example, monthly meeting with a spiritual director)

- Self-direction
  (For example, maintaining a journal)

- Other

Ministry

- Intentional simplification of life
  (For example, mentally testing that each proposed material acquisition be utilized and not just acquired)

- Use of personal resources: talents, finances, energy

- A focus of service (ministry) beyond the church
  (For example, three hours per week service in a soup kitchen)

- A focus of service within the worshiping community

- Social and political commitments

- My life as a model for others
  (For example, a monthly appraisal that such modeling is the case, whether intended or not!)

- Other

This full listing will appear to most readers to be formid-able indeed—and I cannot disagree! Note, however, the recommendation that only a few categories listed be selected for trial. Some years ago, my initial listing included only four or five items that seemed very much needed. As the years passed, however, I began to consider the rule to be more a helpful inventory than a rigid taskmaster, and the number of areas of guidelines have grown even as my fidelity to the listing has increased. More significantly, today I sense that the practice of regular personal inventory seems right for me to continue. My evolution of discovery, acceptance, and use of my inventory followed and I commend consideration of the elements noted:

> I discovered, by trial and error, with the assistance of others, what had helped in the past to give me a sense of well-being and patience with myself and others. Using St. Paul's listing of the fruit of the Spirit (Gal. 5:22f.), I raised the question: Does prac-ticing this particular choice nurture my sense of love, joy, peace, and the dispositions of patience, kindness, goodness, faithfulness, gentleness, and self-control? This insight guided my determination to continue.

> I formalized my discoveries by writing them in a format similar to the one above and kept the list readily available. I found it important that the items be specific. For example, it is far more helpful to say, "I'll do aerobic exercises for one hour three days per week" than to proclaim, "I hope to get this soft body back into shape."

> I observed as I followed my plan how the specifics I had chosen for the various areas could or could not realistically be abided by in everyday life.

I periodically monitored (in a formal way) myself and the person assisting me. The other person ratified what I believed to be true about myself or helped my discovery to be of greater clarity. Obviously, such monitoring is possible only when specific intentions have been chosen.

I modified my guidelines and again committed to record them and keep them at hand for periodic reference.

My conviction is that life is more tranquil with such a set of checkpoints. In addition, discipline has been very liberating, and I can more and more be myself, the one who is still being formed in Christian maturity.

Beginning

One of the surest ways to begin any journey or action is to start. This observation might sound tongue-in-cheek, but it also contains helpful wisdom. I do not know what outcomes readers might experience, but it is evident that life is trial and error throughout. My wife, Norvene, occasionally uses a very simple exercise to help people approach meditation without insisting on outcomes. She suggests that the participants silently count to ten, thinking each number successively with each full breath. If a person is distracted, she or he returns to number one and begins anew. There are very few ten-pointers! Most participants are relieved when she explains that the main idea is not to count all the way to ten but to be able to restart many times while dealing with oneself gently, as meditation requires. But not all participants are relieved. Some at first feel tricked, for to them the point of the exercise is to succeed. I suspect that a few years ago it would not have been a pleasant prospect for me to consider that I might need frequently to return to "square one." Now I can laugh at myself, giving thanks through my chuckles that some important growth might have taken place.

So, then, a beginning. I shall not guess about outcomes, for that would anticipate surprises that are too personal to be anticipated. Each person can do only the best she or he can. John Chapman wrote about prayer in a way that is also helpful to view discipline in all aspects of life.

> First, "Pray as you can, and don't try to pray as you can't!" and second, "The less you pray, the worse it goes."[4]

Gerald May comments on the same discipline.[5]

> If you do pray:
> 1. Pray
> 2. Do the best you can
> 3. Accept the whole situation
> 4. Watch with awe
>
> If you don't pray:
> 1. Do the best you can
> 2. Accept the whole situation
> 3. Watch with awe
>
> If you can't pray:
> 1. Do the best you can
> 2. Accept the whole situation
> 3. Watch with awe
> 4. Be still and listen

Both sets of advice apply to all of life, not only to prayer.

Notes

Chapter 1

1 Karl Albrecht, *Stress and the Manager: Making It Work for You* (New York: Prentice-Hall, 1979), 47.

2 Pressure is used here simply to signify the external or internal forces that are perceived to make some demand upon a person.

3 Walter McQuade and Ann Aikman, *Stress: How to Stop Your Mind Killing Your Body* (London: Arrow Books, 1974).

4 The definition of stress is discussed in chapter 7, "The Dissection of Stress," of Hans Selye's *The Stress of Life* (New York: McGraw-Hill, 1956). Briefly, stress is the body's nonspecific response to any demand made upon it.

5 The sympathetic nervous system is one of two major subsystems of the human involuntary (autonomic) nervous system. The sympathetic system generally expends energy and readies the body for action (e.g., by increasing heartbeat or respiration rates at the time of perceived danger).

6 The parasympathetic nervous system is one of two major subsystems of the human involuntary (autonomic) nervous system. The parasympathetic system generally conserves energy and restores the body to normal conditions (e.g., reducing heartbeat or respiration rates).

7 For much of this discussion I am indebted to Hans Selye, *The Stress of Life*.

8   Hans Selye, "Confusion and Controversy in the Stress Field," *Journal of Human Stress*, Vol. 1, 2d printing (June 1975): 37–44. Eustress is a physiologic reaction of the body that gives a sense of goodness, excitement, or well-being. For example, a person might experience eustress in the midst of witnessing a stirring athletic contest or after successfully dealing with the challenge of a weather crisis, although the person might have felt pressured at the time.

9   Hans Selye, *Stress Without Distress* (New York: J. B. Lippincott, 1974), 85.

Chapter 2

1   Herbert Freudenberger, *Burn-Out* (Garden City, N.Y.: Doubleday, 1980), 13.

2   Wayne E. Oates, *Pastoral Psychology* 19, no. 187 (October 16, 1968): 16.

3   Gerald May, "Sabbath for the Brain," *Shalem News* 9, no. 2 (May 1985): 5.

4   Jillie Collins, "Measuring up to the Stress," *The Guardian*, Manchester, England (August 26, 1986): 8.

5   Adrian van Kaam, *Formative Spirituality*, vol. I entitled *Fundamental Formation* (New York: Crossroad, 1983). Extensive work at the Institute of Formative Spirituality (Duquesne University, Pittsburgh, Penn.) is concerned with the emerging science of human formation. Van Kaam asserts the importance of learning to value formative thinking as well as informative thinking. "Since everything in life and world can serve our unfolding, formative thinking can point to one possible, universal way of thought that can be applied to all things in our lives. Informative thinking, on the contrary, tends to be more issue-oriented than formation-oriented"(xvii).

6   Generally following the view of Adrian van Kaam, four sources of energy that continue to give shape to ongoing life are: vital, which originates in the biological forces that animate all persons; cultural, which is received from human communities; functional, which is derived from participation in activity; and transcendent, which leads us to energy beyond what can perceived by the senses. These are the formative dimensions of life.

7   The journal *Studies on Formative Spirituality* (Pittsburgh) contains many references to these dynamics in the 1980 issues and later.

8 *New Oxford Annotated Bible, Revised Standard Version* (New York: Oxford University Press, 1977), Eccl. 3:11; hereafter cited as RSB.

9 May, "Sabbath for the Brain," 5.

10 Functionalism is a dominance of doing in life, often to the exclusion of health-giving contributions from culture, other persons, the divine, and our own bodies.

Chapter 3

1 Martin Buber, *Moses* (Oxford: East & West Library, 1946), 20–32, 145.

2 David and Evelyn Whitehead, *Method in Ministry* (New York: Seabury Press, 1980). See especially chapter 10, "A Christian Asceticism of Time," for the development of this idea.

3 Augustine of Hippo, *Confessions*, Book 11, as quoted by J. A. Gunn in the *Problem of Time* (London: George Allen and Utwin Ltd., 1929), 17.

Chapter 4

1 Dorothy L. Sayers, *Unpopular Opinions* (London: Victor Gollancz Ltd., 1946), 122.

2 David W. Torrance and Thomas F. Torrance, eds., *Calvin's Commentaries: The First Epistle of Paul the Apostle to the Corinthians,* trans. John W. Fraser (Grand Rapids, Mich.: William B. Eerdmans Publishing Co., 1960), 153.

3 David Attwood, *The Spade and the Thistle* (Nottingham, England: Grove Books Ltd., 1980), 13.

4 Timothy Fry, ed., *The Rule of St. Benedict* (Collegeville, Minn.: The Liturgical Press, 1980), 243.

5 Mark Twain, *The Adventures of Tom Sawyer* (New York: Greenwich House, 1982), 19.

6 *Webster's New Collegiate Dictionary*, eighth edition (Springfield, Mass.: G. & C. Merriam Company, 1980), 1340.

7 Jean Kinkead Martine, "Working for a Living," *A Way of Working,* ed. D. M. Dowling (New York: Parabola Books, 1986), 60.

Chapter 5

1 Rollo May, recorded in my journal.

2 Phil. 3:20 (*New American Bible*), "We have citizenship in heaven," St. Paul wrote in a letter to the young church at Philippi (some translations read "commonwealth" instead of "citizenship"). But I do not want to enter into a discussion of the many views of heaven.

3 *New American Bible* (Nashville: Thomas Nelson Bible Publishers, 1971); hereafter cited as NAB.

4 I credit the use of the word original in this context to Adrian van Kaam, especially in *The Search for Spiritual Identity* (Denville, N.J.: Dimension Books, 1975). See also "Spirituality and Originality" in *Studies in Formative Spirituality* 1, no. 1 (February 1980), 7. The original person may be viewed as the self made possible and brought forth by God at birth while remaining partly hidden in the divine Creator. Confrontation with this mystery often begins for an individual in the search for a life mission. A helpful question might be: Who am I to be? The ensuing lifelong search is described by Dag Hammarskjold:

> At every moment you choose yourself. But do you choose your self? Body and soul contain a thousand possibilities from which you can build many I's. But in only one is there a congruence of the elector and the elected. Only one—which you will never find until you have excluded all superficial and fleeting possibilities of being and doing with which you toy, out of curiosity or wonder or greed, and which hinder you from casting anchor in the experience of the mystery of life, and the consciousness of the talent entrusted to you which is yours. (*Markings* [New York: Alfred A. Knopf, 1966], 19.)

5 Formative experiences are encounters that, often upon and because of thoughtful consideration, significantly influence the direction, choices, and valuing of one's ongoing life.

6 We might speculate that not only past events and influences but also the future and all it holds have a direct relationship to the person I presently am, that the person I am being urged to become intrudes into the present. That is a topic for another setting, but it does suggest that the person whom God enables me to be in the future is not different from the original creation.

7 George Matheson, "O Love That Will Not Let Me Go," no. 458 in *The Hymnal 1940* (New York: The Church Hymnal Corporation, 1961).

8   Francis Thompson, *The Hound of Heaven* (London: Burns and Oates Ltd., 1913).

9   C. S. Lewis, *The Weight of Glory and Other Addresses* (New York: Macmillan, 1949), 6–16.

Chapter 6

1   See Matt. 12, Mark 3, Luke 6, and John 7–11.

2   Abraham Heschel, *I Asked for Wonder,* ed. Samuel H. Dresner (New York: Crossroad, 1983), 36.

Chapter 7

1   Walt Whitman, "A Song of Myself," *An Anthology of Famous English and American Poetry*, ed. William Rose Benet and Conrad Aiken (New York: The Modern Library, 1944), 664.

2   Reflection is used here primarily to mean a gentle recollection and pondering or meditating on matters associated with our lives and life settings, notably about persons, objects, events, memories, feelings, and aspirations that are sensed to have an impact on our lives, no matter how great or slight that impact might be. More briefly, simple reflection is a thoughtful dwelling on concrete life situations.

3   *New English Bible* (Cambridge: Cambridge University Press, 1970), Luke 2:19; hereafter cited as NEB.

4   Introspection is an inward examination of one's own thoughts and feelings. In contrast, transcendent reflection is used here to suggest that one's meditation not cease with the process of analytic introspection, but that both personal involvement in it and any insights or conclusions resulting therefrom be released or handed on to the Transcendent One.

5   "What creates continuity in life is not particular acts as such. The secret of life's cohesion seems to reside in a flexible constellation of lasting dispositions that form the foundation of these acts. Together they dispose us to act coherently and in tune with the direction we have chosen to follow." Adrian van Kaam, *Formative Spirtuality,* vol. 2: *Human Formation* (New York: Crossroad, 1985), 1. The entire second volume of van Kaam's five-volume series is devoted to an exploration of the dispositional base of life as a person experiences it.

Chapter 8

1   Josef Pieper, *About Love,* trans. Richard and Clara Winston (Chicago: Franciscan Herald Press, 1974), 26.

2   Formative memory consists of reminders and reflection from a person's past experiences that continue to influence the present and future direction of life's course. Adrian van Kaam discusses the concept in several writings, most notably in *Fundamental Formation,* 302.

3   The Ignatian Exercises are a plan of systematic meditation and prayer typically used in directed retreats for persons seeking to decide on a state of life or to deepen their Christian commitment. They were originally written in a four-week format by St. Ignatius of Loyola in the sixteenth century.

4   An examination of conscience is a systematic scrutiny of personal faults and shortcomings that burden an individual. "The spiritual losses and gains of the past year are meditated on in order that the *fundamental attitudes* underlying the faults and failures may be discovered and altered. [The] dust of routine is to be blown away, a new understanding sought of the less obviously false principles around which a multitude of apparently disparate faults tend to cluster." (Robert W. Gleason, introduction to *The Spiritual Exercises of St. Ignatius,* trans. Anthony Mottola [Garden City, N.Y.: Doubleday, 1964], 28.)

5   Basil Hume, *Searching for God* (London: Hodder and Stoughton, 1977), 117.

6   Nikos Kazantzakis, *Zorba the Greek* (New York: Simon & Schuster, 1952), 120.

7   John A. T. Robinson, *Truth is Two-Eyed* (Philadelphia: Westminster, 1979), 4–17.

Chapter 9

1   Spiritual formation is a process that involves personal search for some unique form of life. Christian spiritual formation involves values and practices that foster our becoming more and more in the image of Christ—necessarily retaining those practices that nurture and relinquishing those that are toxic to the ongoing unfolding of that uniqueness (uniqueness more narrowly referring to the original person).

2   *The Book of Common Prayer* (The Church of England, 1662) (Cambridge: Cambridge University Press), 294.

3 *The Book of Common Prayer* (The Episcopal Church) (New York: Seabury, 1979), 858.

4 Alexander Schemann, *The World as Sacrament* (New York: Herder & Herder, 1965).

5 Jean-Pierre de Caussade, *Self-Abandonment to Divine Providence*, trans. Algard Thorwold (London: Burns Oates & Washbourne Ltd., 1933). Self-abandonment to divine providence is the voluntary yielding of the course of one's life to God, neither asking for nor refusing anything in advance. The emphasis is on *self*-abandonment.

6 Jean-Pierre de Caussade, *The Sacrament of the Present Moment*, trans. Kitty Muggeridge (San Francisco: Harper & Row, 1982).

7 Caussade, *Self-Abandonment*, 3.

8 Ibid., 18.

9 Ibid., 51.

10 Ibid., 11.

11 John Chapman, *The Spiritual Letters of Dom John Chapman*, trans. Roger Huddleston (London: Sheed and Ward, 1944), 155.

12 "To find God as good in the tiniest and most ordinary events as in the greatest is to have no ordinary but a great and extra-ordinary faith" (Caussade, *Self-Abandonment*, 29).

13 His reasoning for this is that "the crosses sent them by Providence, with which their state of life supplies them at every moment, open to them a far surer and swifter path than extra-ordinary states and works." (Ibid., xxi.)

14 Ibid., 44. In the more recent Muggeridge translation, the words are, "The present moment holds infinite riches beyond your wildest dreams" (Muggeridge, *Sacrament*, 82).

15 Caussade, *Self-Abandonment*, 43.

16 Ibid., 44.

17 Ibid., xiii. *Letters* is the only book published by Caussade. It was published anonymously in 1741 as *Spiritual Instructions in the form of Dialogues concerning different Methods of Prayer.*

18 Ibid.

19 *The Book of Common Prayer* (The Episcopal Church), 127.

20 J. B. Leishman, *The Metaphysical Poets* (Oxford: Clarendon Press, 1934), 168.

21 Ibid.

Chapter 10

1 Edward Malatesta, introduction to Jacquet Guillet et al, *Discernment of Spirits* (Collegeville, Minn.: The Liturgical Press, 1970), 9.

2 Adrian van Kaam, *In Search of Spiritual Identity* (Denville, N.J.: Dimension Books, 1975), 109.

3 Jerome Lawrence and Robert E. Lee, *Auntie Mame* (New York: Dramatists Play Service, Inc., 1956), 90. The deletion is mine.

4 C. S. Lewis, *The Weight of Glory and Other Essays* (New York: Macmillan, 1949), 4.

5 Adrian van Kaam, *On Being Yourself* (Denville, N.J.: Dimension Books, 1972), 144–47.

6 Leslie Farber, *The Ways of the Will* (New York: Basic Books, 1966), 7–10.

7 Ibid., 15.

8 Van Kaam, *On Being Yourself*, 147.

9 Paul Ricouer, *Phenomenology of Will and Action,* ed. E. W. Strauss (Pittsburgh: Duquesne University Press, 1967), 14.

10 Ibid., 24.

11 Ibid., 56f.

Chapter 11

1 Francis Baur, *Life in Abundance: A Contemporary Spirituality* (New York: Paulist Press, 1983), 9.

2 I have previously used the word *disposition* in commenting about the interior characteristic or temperament of patience that may become more natural as we practice it, and thereby predispose ourselves so that there is an increasing likelihood that our prereflective responses to situations will be made patiently rather than impatiently.

3 Jean-Pierre de Caussade, *Self-Abandonment to Divine Providence*, trans. Algar Thorwold (London: Burns, Oates & Washbourne Ltd., 1933), xiii.

4 Ibid., xvi.

5 Robert Bellah, Richard Madsen, William M. Sullivan, Ann Swidler, Steven M. Tipton, *Habits of the Heart* (Berkeley: University of California Press, 1985).

6 Tilden Edwards, *Sabbath Time* (New York: The Seabury Press, 1982), 3.

Chapter 12

1 "No Earthly Good," J. R. Cash, recorded by the Oak Ridge Boys (New York: Columbia Records, 1976).

2 Stability, obedience, and conversion of life are essentially three closely related aspects of full commitment to monastic life. Stability signifies more than geographical fixity within a community and includes a willingness to persevere, even when obedience seems difficult. Conversion of life has been described in several ways over the centuries but overall seems to mean fidelity to monastic life in community.

3 Esther de Waal, *Seeking God* (Collegeville, Minn.: The Liturgical Press, 1984), 85.

4 John Chapman, *The Spiritual Letters of Dom John Chapman, O.S.B.*, trans. Roger Huddleston (London: Sheed & Ward, 1944), 25.

5 Gerald May, *Simply Sane: The Spirituality of Mental Health* (New York: Crossroad, 1977), 113.

Index

Idolatry, 21
Ignatian Exercises, 90, 166n
Impersonality, 3
Individuality, distinction between originality and, 139–40
Inductive reasoning, 65
Informative thinking, 162n
Inner necessity, concept of, 129
Intentional reflection, purpose of, 79–80
Intercession, 149
Introspection, 165n
Isaiah, 133

Jeremiah, 54–55, 72
Jesus Christ
    and concept of Sabbath, 67–68
    healings of, 68
Jesuits, Ignatian Exercises of, 90
Job, 43, 45
John the Baptist, 133
Journaling, 33, 89, 150–53

Kairos, 28–29, 31–32, 33, 34
    distinguishing between chronos and, 33
Knowles, David, 105–6, 138

Labor, religious views of, 37–42
Lewis, C. S., 59–60
Life, decisions on responding to, 115–16
Life dimensions, 162n
    cultural, 15, 16, 17, 58, 162n
    functional, 16, 17–19, 58, 162n
    transcendent, 16–17, 58, 112, 162n
    vital, 15, 16, 17, 58, 112, 162n
Life disciplines, inventorying, 155, 156–57
Life experiences, on work, 43
Life planning, 137–38
    conflicts in, 137
    importance of communication in, 137–38

Life settings, presence to own, 91–93
Life situation, analyzing one's, 51
Life style, analyzing personal, 20–22
Listening, 119, 120, 143, 145–46
Living, time-centered, 26–30
Love, 147
    concept of, 68
Luke, 76–77, 126

Management by objectives (MBO), 135–36
    personal use of, 136
Mark, 95, 133
Mary, Blessed Virgin, 76–78, 80, 150
Matrimony, Holy, 102, 107, 108
Matthew, 92, 118, 144
May, Gerald, 12–13, 160
May, Rollo, 50
Meditation, 159
Merton, Thomas, 25
Minisabbath, 112
Monastic communities, attitude toward work in, 40–41
Monastic stability, Benedictine vow of, 92
Moving, temptation to keep, 50–52

Nehemiah, 72
"No," learning to say, 63
Nuns of the Visitation, 103

Obedience
    Benedictine vow of, 154, 169n
    and upward repression, 125–26
Objects
    presence to, 93–94
    as sacrament, 109
Openness to conversion of life, Benedictine vow of, 154
Ordination, 102
Original, 164n